THE RAINBOW EFFECT

KATHLYN GAY

THE RAINBOW EFFECT

INTERRACIAL FAMILIES

Franklin Watts
New York / London / Toronto / Sydney
1987

All photographs, except for the one on page 79,
are by the author

Photograph on page 79 is courtesy of
Ed and Joan Broadfield

Library of Congress Cataloging-in-Publication Data

Gay, Kathlyn.
The rainbow effect.

Bibliography: p.
Includes index.
Summary: Uses interviews with members of
interracial/interethnic families to explore problems
faced by "mixed" children in such areas as family,
school, dating, and adoption.
1. Children of interracial marriage—United States—
Juvenile literature. 2. Interracial marriage—United
States—Juvenile literature. [1. Interracial marriage]
I. Title.
HQ777.9.G39   1987   306.8′46   86-26689
ISBN 0-531-10343-9

CONTENTS

To Ben E. Barnes,

*whose color difference
has made a
profound difference
in my life and
whose understanding of
human commonalities
has helped him effect
positive changes in
his community.*

K.G.

THE RAINBOW EFFECT

INTRODUCTION

"Children of the Rainbow" is how *Newsweek* described the offspring of interracial couples in a 1984 article about the way biracial young people cope with "mixed" heritages. Until the 1980s, very few national magazines or other publications focused on the positive as well as problematic aspects of interracial families. The subject has, for the most part, been taboo, unless the emphasis happened to be on the "exotic" or "erotic" nature of interracial unions. "Ordinary people" of mixed heritage—interracial families with middle-class values and ways of life—were ignored, as though such family structures could not possibly exist.

Since 1975, I have been talking informally or conducting structured interviews with members of "ordinary" interracial/interethnic families. My interest was prompted in part by the fact that my Caucasian family includes extended family members of various cultural groups. In addition, I have often discussed interracial and interethnic issues with business partners—Ben and Leona Barnes, a black couple who have long been close friends of our family; their children and our children (now grown) consider both homes their own.

Ben Barnes, who has collaborated on several other books with me, provided special assistance for the early research and recent follow-up interviews for this work. Some of the interviews came about because of our appearances on dozens of TV and radio talk shows in such cities as Milwaukee, Chicago, Detroit, Cleveland, and New York. During that research we often were asked (by those who otherwise claimed to accept interracial/ interethnic unions) the loaded question: "But what about the children?" I believe that question should be countered with, "What *about* the children?" Why the concern for "mixed" children if there is not already a labeling process going on—a process that marks all people "of color" in a prejudicial manner?

In my view, most children and adults "of the rainbow" are as varied and as individualistic as any other members of our society. Most appear to be functioning in a positive manner. But they do so in spite of many obstacles thrown in their paths via institutionalized racism.

This book was not written to advocate interracial or interethnic unions. But it was written to present the view that interracial/interethnic families have much to offer our so-called American way of life. Family members also have much to say about what it means to appreciate differences as well as commonalities of the human race.

Kathlyn Gay

WHO AM I?

1

*I am not here to beg and plead
with this racist society for a
racial identity. I already have
a place—an interracial place.
I already have an identity—
an interracial identity. I exist.
I am real. I am here. And I no
longer feel that it is so much
my responsibility to remind
society of these facts, as it
is this society's responsibility
to simply recognize me.*

Bess Martinson
(from I-Pride Readings, 11/79)

*S*ome of my people call him Chinese—so do kids at the elementary school where Jason goes. But my son is part Cambodian. His daddy, Sok Toeur, is from Cambodia. That's where his people are— or were; a lot of them were killed in the fighting and all." Jason's mother, Ruthie, a sales representative for a lathe and drill company, carefully explained one part of her son's heritage.

Sitting in a family room that she had helped add on to her neat midwestern bungalow, Ruthie said: "We talk a lot about Jason's father. Sok and I separated some time ago, and he's in Louisiana now. Jason doesn't remember anything about his father. But I've always tried to teach my son about his two different backgrounds. He knows about black people, since he's around my family all the time. I have to teach him what I know about Cambodia. Fortunately, we have a Cambodian friend, Heig, who is also a friend of Jason's father. He keeps in touch and we learn about Sok from Heig. I just wish Jason had had a chance to learn a second language—his father speaks seven languages. Sok was just learning English when I met him at an adult education class . . ."

Six-year-old Jason suddenly bounded into the room, a streak of energy. He was carrying a large photo album that almost overwhelmed him. Quickly he flipped the pages to find pictures of himself with his father and mother. "See, here's Sok Toeur," he said, obviously eager to show off his father and to say his name. Jason's round face, dark straight hair and skin color clearly resemble his father's.

"But look here—at the eyes and the rest of his features. He's like me," Ruthie pointed out. "A lot of people don't see that, though. People ask all the time if I've adopted Jason or if I'm taking care of him or something. Then when they find out he's my biological child they begin wondering out loud how Jason is going to think of himself —as black or Chinese—people still can't get it straight about being Cambodian!" Ruthie shook her head and laughed. "It's funny really. I just can't get upset about it! I have enough to do keeping Jason and myself going."

Ruthie is able to brush off the fact that the general public has little understanding of her son's parentage. But she made it clear that she is serious about helping Jason, as he grows and matures, to be proud of his *bi*racial heritage.

It remains to be seen how others outside Jason's immediate circle of family and friends will perceive him. In U.S. Census counts and on some official documents Jason may be labeled "black." If so, he has, in effect, officially been left out of the "Asian" category. If he is called "Asian," he then is denied his black heritage—in official categories anyway.

So which should take precedence—the so-called racial origin of Jason's father? Or should his mother's color category and heritage be the criterion for identification? And how will Jason identify himself later on? As he matures, how will he answer the questions "Who am I?" and "To what group do I belong?"

Perhaps the questions will not be crucial to Jason and he may simply respond with his given and family names. But Jason, like the rest of us, will probably be categorized and classified by others.

One of the most common forms of identification is by national or ethnic group (people sharing the same language and customs) or by color, usually referred to as

Corey Adams (black/white) and Jason Furlow (Cambodian/black)

Corey's mother, Julie, and Jason's mother, Ruthie, help the boys assemble a kite.

"race." However, race is not a scientific term and it can be ambiguous. For example, many Asian-Americans may have Caucasian ancestry, but if their physical characteristics are considered by whites to be more Asian than Caucasian, they will be categorized as part of the "yellow race." A person who is of white and Native American ancestry and, in the Anglo view, appears "Indian" will be labeled as such or of the "red" or "brown" race. Even though most black Americans have some white European ancestry, they are defined as black or Negro. However, throughout most of America's history, "Negro" has had a degrading connotation, since it has been contorted by many whites to the ugly racial slur "nigger."

The white majority view in our society is that people of white European or Anglo-Saxon Protestant (WASP) ancestry are "all white," which in a racist view is a mark of superiority. Thus, racial identification is a tool that the nation's white majority has used to maintain power. An old saying points this out with poignant clarity: "If you're white you're all right, if you're brown stick around, if you're black step back." On the basis of such racist labeling, the majority white society forces anyone of color to lower levels on the status ladder.

Yet, millions of people in this nation share more than a single culture and national or racial heritage. Throughout the history of humankind, people of different colors and national origins have intermarried or formed interracial unions and produced offspring who represent a combination of inherited traits. And racial mixing has been part of our nation's history since its beginning. But only in very recent times has there been much rational discussion about interracial families. In fact, the subject is often treated with disdain by much of the white majority.

Negative attitudes about interracial families usually stem from the white supremacist beliefs just described— the idea that a "pure" white race must be maintained, even though Caucasians have long mixed with people of color. This was especially true during slavery when white men forced themselves on black women, producing countless "mixed" offspring. Black women could be bearers of slaves but were not allowed to form partnerships that could be dignified by marriage. At the same time, black men could be severely punished or killed if they were merely suspected of sexual alliances with white women.

Even after the Civil War, most states passed laws that banned marriages between blacks and whites. Those laws stayed "on the books" for many decades. Not until 1967 did the Supreme Court rule that such laws are unconstitutional. As Chief Justice Earl Warren wrote in his decision: "Under our Constitution, the freedom to marry or not marry a person of another race resides with the individual and cannot be infringed upon by the State."

Another worn argument against interracial marriage that has persisted to this day goes something like this: "If God wanted the races to mix, He wouldn't have created different colors and nations." Other myths couched in religious terms imply that "God prohibits intermarriage." But many religious leaders point out that even the most superficial study of the Bible will show there are no biblical decrees against intermarriage on the basis of skin color, hair, shape of the eyes, or other physical features.

Have attitudes changed over the years? Are interracial or interethnic families more readily accepted by the majority of Americans? The answer is a qualified "somewhat." Acceptance, although limited, may be based on the fact that interracial and interethnic marriages are on the increase, as are the number of "mixed" children. Estimates of the total number of mixed offspring range from hundreds of thousands to more than five million. No firm statistics exist, since there is no official count or way to categorize people of interracial or interethnic ancestry. And many people over the years have been reluctant to claim a mixed heritage because they have feared society's disapproval. As for the interracial or interethnic families today, outside approval often depends on the family ancestry, social and economic status, and where the family lives.

For example, Janet, who is sixteen, and her fourteen-year-old brother, Andrew, are part of an upper middle class interethnic family in southern California. They say they have experienced no discrimination. The teenagers' maternal grandparents are from Mexico and their paternal grandparents are of German ancestry. Family members see themselves as "cross-cultural," but have the appearance of being part of the majority white culture.

Both teenagers say they have close relationships with their extended Mexican family—grandparents, aunts, uncles, cousins—and they take special pride in being part of that family. They have learned from their grandparents, who live nearby, to speak a little Spanish. They also go to fiestas in their community, which has a large Mexican population. Both say they love Mexican food, but it is not the only type of food they enjoy. "We seldom really think of ourselves as *only* Mexican—we're just us," Janet said. "Maybe some people call us Mixed but we're Americans. We do the same things most kids in our school do. I don't see any big deal about having parents with families from two different cultures."

A San Francisco architect, whose parentage includes Japanese-American/black/Seminole Indian/French Caucasian, said he seldom has experienced problems because of his multicultural heritage. He "looks" Japanese, as he pointed out, but his skin tones are much darker than most Japanese-Americans. "Where I live in San Francisco, there are many Japanese-Americans, so I see mirrors of myself in various places," he said. "I feel comfortable with that identity, yet I also have ties with my black heritage, although I'm not categorized that way by whites."

Being categorized as black can create difficulties for a person of biracial ancestry when the black classification is used as a put-down. A staff accountant in Chicago who considers herself "second-generation biracial" explained that her heritage includes Irish, African, and American black/white. Even though her skin color is as light as many of the Caucasians she works with, she is not regarded that way. "Instead, I am labeled black and whenever a job comes up that's in the ghetto, my bosses try to assign it to me," she said. Why? "Because whites are afraid to go into the black neighborhoods. They think I won't have any problems. A rough neighborhood is a rough neighborhood for anyone—no matter what her or his color! Yet, whites in the office ignore my black heritage when they start talking about blacks as a group. I've actually had bosses tell me they were ready to hire prospective employees who were well-qualified but they couldn't because those applicants were black and wouldn't be accepted. It's pure craziness. A sickness."

Black/white biracial people may be faced with still another double bind. Certain black groups, in particular young adolescents, may not readily accept a biracial person who "looks" black but whose behavior and speech patterns are seen as "whitey-white." Sociologist Russell Ellis, University of California, Berkeley, speaks from his own experience and as a black parent of biracial teenagers: "There is a period of time in the growth of some young black women when they become concretely 'tribal'—if you are not obviously black, you are literally ejected from the group. The young black women walk together, 'they be together' and if you are not 'really black' you don't belong," Dr. Ellis said.

Shaum Urquhart, whose mother is white and father is black, agrees that "black girls gave me the most problems" in the northern California high school she attended. Now in her early twenties and teaching preschoolers, Shaum says that when she was in her teens, black girls often accused her of being "stuck up" and seemed to resent the fact that she "talked white" and had "prissy" ways. Shaum added that she "really was sort of prissy as a little girl. And until I was about thirteen or fourteen I didn't want anything to do with being black.

"My parents were divorced," she explained, "and I lived with my mother in a white middle-class neighborhood. I didn't look too different because of my light skin and brown curly hair, although people couldn't figure out my heritage. I remember once someone asked me 'What are you?' and I responded with 'I'm a girl,' thinking I was really clever. But my face turned beet-red because I realized then I was trying to hide my biracialness and at the same time was denying my father, whom I love very much. Fortunately, I started spending time with black relatives and friends who helped me see it is okay to be black. Now I can readily say 'Yes, I'm black, and yes, I'm white.' I feel I have the ability to identify either way and I *like* being biracial."

Being able to associate with people who represent both sides of a biracial person's heritage is an important factor in finding identity. Isolation often leads to confusion and discomfort. As Lindi, a black/white biracial teenager in Indiana explained: "I go to a rural school that is mostly white and I'm uncomfortable because I'm different from everyone else in the school." Rather shy and soft-spoken, Lindi pointed out that there were children of two black families in her school, but she didn't know them well because they were younger. "Anyhow, I wouldn't get along with them just because I'm part black. They know who they are and I know I'm Mixed, but sometimes it's really hard to know what I should call myself," she said.

Such a dilemma is voiced by many parents of "rainbow" children—the most recent jargon for offspring of interracial couples. In fact, there is an ongoing debate among interracial families across the nation with regard to the proper terminology to describe a person's dual-race heritage. In the opinion of Charles Stewart, Jr., a minister and director of a support group for interracial families in

*"I know I'm Mixed, but sometimes it's really hard
to know what I should call myself."—Lindi Hicks,
age 15. (Lindi's brother, Austin, at right, is also
Mixed. Their mother, Connie, at left, is white; her
former husband was black. Connie's second husband,
Gene, who is white, has adopted Lindi and Austin.)*

Tarentum, Pennsylvania, such a classification as biracial
(or even tri- or quad-) defines "an individual's inherited
human blend of two or more races." As a black father of
biracial children himself, Rev. Stewart believes that *biracial* correctly describes his "rainbow" children. "*Biracial,*
as a term, also acknowledges both parents—myself and
my wife, the children's mother, who is white," Rev. Stewart
said.

Still, some interracial parents dislike the term *biracial.*
As one father put it: "*Biracial* just sounds too scientific—
somehow inhuman." He and many other interracial parents prefer such terms as *tan, brown, mixed,* or *interracial*
if their children have to be categorized. Yet, there is a

danger, as a number of interracial couples have pointed out, in making too much out of classifications. "No one wants to have a situation like that of South Africa, where people are labeled and classified according to fine distinctions between color differences," said Shaun Shields, a biracial adult of black/Chinese/white ancestry, living in San Francisco. Shaun believes it is absurd that our society forces a biracial person into a category, usually that of the minority parent. "If I had a Swedish and French ancestry, I would not be pushed into being one or the other," he noted.

Most biracial people want to find their own identity and not be forced to fit images that others have defined for them. Yet, there are many contradictions and pitfalls as adolescents try to define who they are and as parents try to guide their biracial children. Color labels certainly do not describe the actual skin color of any person. No white person, for example, has pure white skin. Rather, the skin tones might range from light pink to various beige or dark tan hues. People categorized as black have skin tones ranging from ebony to ecru to pinkish shades. So very young children may become confused by color labels, especially if the children are labeled black and can see that their skin tones are really "tan," "brown," or some other shade.

In some interracial families, parents may insist, as their children are developing, that race and color are not important to emphasize, but such distinctions are constantly made in our society, usually in a derogatory way. So children have to be taught that "being black" or "being Japanese" or "being Cherokee" is a matter of being proud of belonging to a cultural group. Ethnic/racial pride is a factor in building defenses against the negative attitudes about people of color that the majority of white society imposes. But the question for interracial and interethnic parents is how to help their children find an identity that reflects their dual heritage.

Geoff Geiger, who edits a newsletter for I-Pride, a San Francisco–based interracial/intercultural support group, recently pointed out how his thinking has changed on matters of racial identity. Writing for the *I-Pride News-letter*, Geoff explained that since he is white and his wife is black, he thought when his daughter was born in 1984 that she would be simply categorized as "human."

Now, however, Geoff is "no longer so certain." He writes that his daughter "will be considered black in this society, regardless of how her parents view her or how she views herself. And yet, she has a lot of contact with both my side of the family and her mother's, and she will be culturally black *and* white. It seems to me that to merely label her 'black' is not an accurate reflection of her true identity and it angers me that my own heritage is blotted out in society's view of my daughter's back-ground."[1]

Bob and Kathleen Johnson have had similar concerns regarding their biracial offspring, Audra and Chad, now in their teens. "Ten years ago, when our children were preschool age, we were instilling the idea that our chil-dren should be *themselves*," explained Kathleen, whose family ancestry is Cherokee/black. "I remember a long time ago getting a census form and I absolutely refused to put down 'black' as a category for the children. That would be denying their father. But they are not white, either. We have always said the children are Mixed."

Bob, of German ancestry, is a high school teacher in the conservative northern Indiana community in which the Johnsons have lived since the early 1970s. He noted that he and Kathleen have tried to help their children "develop positive self-images, to provide them with security and a healthy outlook toward life. In other words, we have made it a practice to deal with problems as they have come up, not try to anticipate what might happen around each cor-ner. As a result, I think the kids have good self-esteem— they know who they are."

*"Once when I told a new person at school
that my mom is black and my dad is white,
he just jumped back and went 'si-i-ke!'"*
*—Chad Johnson, age 17. (Chad's mother,
Kathleen, is at far right; his sister,
Audra, is on the left, and their father,
Bob, is at far left.)*

No doubt about it, according to Audra, who was pre-
paring for a summer European tour with the school band.
"If anyone ever asks—and a few people have—whether
I'm black or white, I just tell them I'm a chocolate and
vanilla swirl! Some of my friends say they always think of
me as white, though. I guess I do lean more toward white
because our neighborhood is practically all-white, but I
go to an integrated school and have both white and black
friends."

Chad, a couple of years older than his sister and perhaps a shade or so lighter in skin tone, said, "Most of the
kids at school think I'm white." But he pointed out that his

teammates on the school track team and all his friends know he's mixed. "Once when I told a new person at school that my mom is black and my dad is white, he just jumped back and went 'si-i-ke!'—meaning he thought I was psyching him out—not giving him the straight story. Then he was sort of impressed with the idea that I'm mixed."

Many biracial young people report that they have experienced this type of "unique" status, a status that sometimes suggests a biracial person is "exotic" or a "curiosity." Some biracial children, especially those who live in predominately white areas, may be subjected to a "fishbowl" treatment such as twelve-year-old Chandree described.

"When we lived out in the country, kids were always asking me about my color. 'How come you're so dark,' they'd say. And I'd tell them I was out in the sun too long!" Chandree laughed with obvious delight.

"She was the only nonwhite kid in the township," explained Chandree's mother, Ann, who is director of a social-service program in the same community in which the Johnsons live. "People were curious, I guess. They acted like they'd never seen a dark-skinned person before."

Did it bother Chandree that people asked questions about her color?

"Sometimes," she said, a quick frown wrinkling her smooth coffee-and-cream complexion. Then she flashed a mischievous smile. "You know what I did that last summer we lived in the country? I was out in the sun a lot and one of my arms got darker than the other. So when somebody asked me about my color I held up one arm like this and said, 'This is my black side and the other is my white side.' Then I told them my dad's black and my mom's white, so that makes me mixed. Okay?"

So that settled it, right? Not exactly. Chandree said she made a lot of friends at the rural consolidated school but that "some of the kids didn't like me too well. Once all the girls in my class were invited to a birthday party, but this girl who was having the party said her mom said

*"I've got the best of my mom and the best of
my dad. It's the neatest part about being biracial."
—Chandree, age 12. (Chandree with her mother, Ann)*

she could only invite ten girls. There were only twelve in our class. So she didn't ask me. I felt really bad for a while. But you know what? I decided if I ever had a party, I'd invite everybody!"

"She had it rough at first out in the boonies," her mother said. "We wanted to be out in the country so we could raise horses. Chandree likes to ride. But after three years we moved back to town. I felt we needed to be around more black people."

"People out in the country just never met anyone who's black—or mixed," Chandree said, as if to excuse any difficulties she may have experienced in a rural setting.

"Yes, that's what I've taught her," Ann agreed.

What else has Chandree been taught?

"That I've got the best of my mom and the best of my dad. It's the neatest part about being biracial," she said proudly. "It's who I am!"

"IN BLACK AND WHITE"

2

*When I talked to my young children
about their color mixture, I used
the example of coffee and cream.
When we looked at the coffee I
explained it is somewhat my color,
then we poured in the cream,
which is somewhat daddy's color,
we got a nice tan mixture—
my children's color.*

A mother of biracial children

The family moved into the Galewood neighborhood of northwest Chicago. Charles, a professional, had grown up in that all-white section of the city. He was returning to his boyhood home to help care for an elderly aunt. His parents, who had owned the home, had both died.

"I felt I knew the people in the neighborhood, but I guess I was wrong about them," Charles said. He was referring to the way his neighbors reacted when he was joined by his wife, Suzette, a black woman, and their young son.

The first indication of trouble was a threat that came through the mail. GET OUT BEFORE WE BURN YOU OUT, the note said, and was signed: "Area People."

The couple had no intention of running, but they did send their son to stay with friends. The next day, a Sunday, someone threw a piece of concrete through one pane of their front window. The glass had not yet been replaced when the next incident happened.

It was late at night. Charles noticed a man and woman standing in front of his home. The two seemed to be arguing. Then the woman pulled the man away, yelling, "Don't do it! Don't do it!"

Feeling somewhat relieved, Charles and Suzette went to bed and were able to get to sleep. But not for long. They were awakened around 3:00 A.M. by shattering glass. A gasoline-filled beer bottle, better known as a Molotov cocktail, came flying through the window, setting fire to curtains and furniture. Charles put out the blaze, and police finally came to watch the couple's house. But no arrests were ever made.

Reports on the harassment and threats to this interracial family made the wire services and headlines in major newspapers in 1976. Unhappily, that type of attack has not been an isolated incident in the nation during the past two decades—a time, ironically, when our nation has been moving toward a more integrated society. Some black/white interracial families and black families still are subjected to abuse when they move into "all white" neighborhoods, not only in Chicago, but in other cities. In November 1985, for example, an Associated Press story[2] from Philadelphia noted:

> Police officers remained on guard today outside the homes of a black family and an interracial couple in a neighborhood disrupted for two nights by white protesters' shouts of "We want them out," and "Move, move, move." About 300 whites, including a core group of fifty to seventy-five young people, demonstrated Thursday night outside the home of a black man and his white wife. Mounted police cordoned off two and one half blocks on either side of the row houses in the southwest Philadelphia neighborhood. Wednesday night, about 400 people demonstrated a few blocks away, outside the home of a black couple. Police said there was no violence at either demonstration.

Why should black/white and black families be singled out for demonstrations when federal laws clearly state that families cannot be denied housing on the basis of their color, creed, or national origin? Although legal barriers to outright discrimination in housing, jobs, education, and use of public facilities are gone, institutionalized racism still exists. In other words, the majority practice of racial labeling to maintain "white supremacy" (as described earlier) carries over to many aspects of daily living in our society. So does the white stereotypical notion about dark-skinned people being "poor," "lazy," "dirty," and "immoral."

Some parents of biracial youngsters have been subjected to a variety of incidents that reflect others' deeply felt revulsion for interracial families. Black/white interracial families may be victims of public scorn—strangers may stare at, curse, or even physically attack some interracial family members. One white mother walking along a Chicago street with her black/white biracial child was spit on by a passerby and told to get herself and her "nigger kid" out of the area. Another white mother reported that she always kept a picture of her black/white biracial daughter on her desk in the office where she works. But she arrived at the job one morning to find the photo gone. On her desk instead was a picture of a baby ape.

The color question seems to bring out the worst kind of bigotry among some hospital personnel when biracial children are born. A white mother in the Midwest reported that the birth experience with her first biracial child was devastating. "The nurses in the delivery room knew I was going to have a Mixed baby and one nurse told me I deserved to suffer pain. 'Maybe that will teach you a lesson and you won't come back in here again!' she told me. That nurse wouldn't even give me a glass of water, unless I begged for it."

In Gary, Indiana, a black mother whose children are black/Puerto Rican said that she almost had to fight to see her daughter in the hospital after she was born. "My husband and I went to the nursery to view our baby and the nurse wouldn't bring her to us—she insisted the child wasn't ours because she was so light-skinned and I'm dark. Then when I got ready to go home, they messed around for three hours, checking numbers and records and trying to say my daughter wasn't my daughter and they weren't going to let me leave the hospital with her. Finally, I just said 'I'm taking my baby and going home!' "

A number of black/white interracial couples reported during interviews for this book that they have been questioned about being the legitimate parents of offspring who were much lighter or darker in skin tone. The story that Amy (white) and Davon (black) tell is just one example:

It was a balmy Saturday afternoon and Davon was taking his son, Jay, who is as light-skinned as his mother, out to get an ice-cream cone. Davon had driven only a few blocks when two white police officers in a squad car pulled him over. One of them yelled: "Nigger, what are you doing with that little white boy?"

When Davon claimed his child, the officer continued with the harassment: "Look, nigger, that's not your son. You're black, the kid's white!" Davon was forced to get out of the car, accused of kidnapping, and threatened with arrest. "I'm going to radio the station and if there are any missing kids, you're going in with us until somebody comes down to claim this boy and says you have permission to have him," the officer said.

The police could find no reason to hold Davon but decided to escort him home to see if anyone there could identify him. Of course, Amy was able to set the record straight. "But I was almost hysterical by that time," she said. "They'd been gone for over an hour and then when they appeared with the police I couldn't believe I had to identify my son and my son's father! What would have happened had it been a white man driving in a car with a black boy? Would they have been stopped?" Amy wondered aloud.

Perhaps a white parent with a black child would have been just as suspect. But the reported incidents seem to indicate that dark-skinned parents are more often questioned about their light-skinned children. As one black mother in a metropolitan area reported: "I've had security guards in a department store check me out because my little boy is mixed and is about as blond as a Swede. People just want families to fit a certain image—they're supposed to be like the parent—one kind of people."

Being "one kind of people" has a different meaning, though, for many interracial families and others who see themselves not in terms of a single category but part of a multicultural human race or humankind. One family, the Stanli and John Beckers of Shaker Heights, an affluent suburb of Cleveland, Ohio, is deeply committed to exposing the myths of race and the "color coding" that results. In 1984, the Beckers, including their five children then ranging in age from seven through fourteen, presented their philosophy of being human in a heartwarming, articulate collection of essays titled *All Blood Is Red . . . All Shadows Are Dark!*

In a preface to the book, John Becker explained that he is "recognized as 'white' in traditional American color coding," while his wife, Stanli Becker, "is called 'black,' even though her graham-cracker-colored skin is not purely of black African origins." This is just the beginning of an attempt to show that the Becker parents and their children do not fit into the commonly accepted racial categories. Their skin colors range from ebony to ivory, with dark brown and several shades of tan in between.

"This medley of colors is possible, in our case, both because of our 'interracial' marriage and because four of our five children are adopted," John wrote. He went on to explain that as a family they have rejected *race* as a term to classify people, unless the term refers to the human race. The Beckers also deliberately planned to reverse traditional role patterns in parenting and earning a living. John, a former education professor, now stays home to care for the children and handle household duties, while Stanli, the wage earner, is the director of a Cuyahoga Community College youth development program.

The Beckers have made it a point to teach their children about their own individual differences in skin color, hair texture, and other physical features. This was a first step, they believe, to ensure "that our children learned from their earliest days that they are unique, beautiful, and special, and that they do not fit conveniently into color-coded 'racial' categories."[3] Stanli and John have also cautioned their children that others will not think as they do. They have tried to prepare them to deal with racial slurs as well as attempts to put them into racial "boxes."

To provide support for their children, who have been taught to identify themselves as "human," Stanli and John have written a letter addressed to teachers and counselors in their children's schools. The letter, included in the family's book, describes the Becker family philosophy and requests that school personnel respect their children's wish to be called "biracial" or "human" rather than be labeled "black" or "white."

The Beckers have no "grand design" for eliminating racial terms and admit that they, too, have often fallen into the semantic trap of race terminology. But as a family their hope is that they will make a ripple in efforts to set the stage for "true humanness."

There is no way to know how far that "ripple" will spread. Nor is it certain how many people already share the Beckers' view. But the concept has certainly been part of the Byrd family philosophy. Vicki and Hilton Byrd, who are artists, consider themselves citizens of the world and somewhat modern-day gypsies. As Hilton explained it: "You have to know our past to understand our way of life today. We both come from middle-class families in New York City.

"My family is West Indian and we are an incredible range of colors, from blond and blue-eyed to very dark hued. I graduated from Long Island University with a degree in psychology. Vicki is a product of a Jewish mother and father of the so-called white culture. She has an English lit degree from Rutgers. Because of our social concerns, we both got into social work after college, but became disenchanted with that and drove cabs in New York to earn some money. That's how we met—as cab drivers."

"We were both interested in art—and we learned how to work with bronze. We do sculptures and jewelry," Vicki interjected. "And we decided to try to make a living at it. We've traveled to almost every state in the union and through Canada and Mexico exhibiting our work at art shows, fairs, and festivals. But we had to find a 'home base' for our daughter, Quixana, after she got to be school age."

The Byrds picked a small resort community near the Wisconsin and Illinois borders. "We were at an art show there one summer," Vicki explained. "The first thing we noticed was the schooolyard. We saw Asian, black, brown, and white children playing together. That helped us determine we'd settle there, at least for a while."

As the Byrds traveled the continent during the 1970s, they encountered very little antagonism because of the interracial nature of their family. "Perhaps that's because of what we do," Hilton said. "We have been in every kind of community from the very conservative to the most liberal. People usually pay no attention to our color combination. When we are exhibiting, we hold up our charms, so to speak, and people look and buy the decorative things. Then they might do a double take and stay to talk. That's the best part of exhibiting. I admit I'm an integrationist in the broadest sense of the word and I thrive on meeting people, exposing the world to us along with the 'charms' we produce."

While the Byrds experienced no overt disapproval of their mixed family, they often heard people voice concern about mixed children. "Before Quixana came along, I don't know how many times we were asked, 'But what about your children?'"

It's a question that many interracial couples, especially black/white couples, have heard repeatedly. "A lot of people believe that is a legitimate question," say Tom and Susan of Fort Wayne, Indiana, whose four mixed children range in age from their teens to early twenties. "I guess people think that mixing the races is wrong for the kids because they'll have too many hardships, but there is no body of evidence to prove that children of black/white parents suffer any more discrimination or disadvantages than any other youngsters of color," Susan said. "If there are hardships it's because our society still says 'White is right' and labels a black/white mixed child as second-class. I've tried to teach my children to be 'soul conscious,' not 'race conscious.'"

To explain her point, Susan recalled a time when her two daughters were younger. "They were playing hopscotch on the dark- and light-brown floor tiles. The older girl is quite dark, like her father, and she told her little sister, who is lighter—more my color—that she couldn't play on the dark tiles because she wasn't dark enough. Right then and there I sat my daughters down and told them they were not just one color or another. What they are inside is a lot more important. If they see themselves only in terms of color, they limit themselves, put blinders on. It's a prison."

Putting it in somewhat different terms, a respected black businessperson in Chicago and a former Urban League official points out that his long-standing mixed marriage has not produced children who have suffered or who have a race war raging within. "That idea is a lot of crap!" he said bluntly. Of his six children and many grandchildren, he says, "Some are coal black, some yellow, some brown, some white. Everybody gets along. Why shouldn't they?"

Indeed, many black/white interracial families agree that color differences have nothing to do with harmony in a family—or, for that matter, with disagreements. As for psychological problems, Alvin Poussaint, M.D., associate professor of psychiatry at Harvard Medical School, found in his recent study of thirty-seven biracial young people that few suffer from conflicts over which racial group to identify with. He also debunked the myth that biracials have problems getting along with both blacks and whites. Rather, biracial young people appeared to be more open-minded and seldom used racial labels to describe others.[4]

However, the way mixed black/white kids identify is still a matter of controversy for some members of black communities. Using such terms as "part white" or "Mixed" and emphasizing humanness rather than a specific racial category as a way to identify are thought to be denials of a person's black heritage. "It's as if a Mixed person is ashamed of being black," said one young black man. "Anyone who is part black *is* black as far as the rest of the world is concerned, so why not say it? To survive, blacks have to stick together!"

On the other hand, a political activist, Malik Nyerere, who took an African name to signal his heritage, noted that "In the late sixties and seventies, nationalist groups were talking more separateness. We had to do that for racial pride. And some black groups are still so busy hating whitey that they can't see we are in a class struggle —people with power are exploiting minorities, especially the poor among us. Many of us, though, are more concerned today about changes in the economic and political systems of this country. If the power and wealth are shared, there won't be so much emphasis on racial or national loyalty."

Politics and loyalty, however, are not the primary reasons many mixed kids from black/white interracial families identify more strongly with their black heritage. The four teenage daughters of Marcia and Lonnie Banks in Colorado Springs, Colorado, identify primarily as black because that is their choice. Marcia, who is white, says, "We've raised our girls to be proud of who they are and right now they have a social identity as black and are

*"I'm black—no two ways about it.
You can see my mom's white. . . ."
(Ayrica's family: her father, Derek;
brother, Shane; Ayrica; her mother, Monica)*

dating black guys. But they've told me they believe they have the best of both worlds and, as one daughter says, she thinks of herself as a complete person not by a color description only."

Ayrica, a tall, light-tan teenager living in Indiana, is quite clear about her preference: "I'm black—no two ways about it," she said. "You can see my mom's white and so are my grandparents and other relatives on her side. They live close by and I see them a lot. But my dad's people are also in the neighborhood and I've spent a lot of time with them. Dad has a big family. I've just always felt part of it. Mom doesn't get upset about that. Besides, I *think* black—you know? I go to a black church because my grandfather's the preacher there, and I like being in a church where you can get up and get happy. When I'm at grandmama's, she cooks the southern black way— greens, cornbread, chitlins. Mom can do it, too, but it's not quite the same. I hang around with black kids most of the time, too. We're into rapping and stuff. 'Course, white kids do that, too. I don't know. I just like being black."

WHAT'S IN A NAME?

3

The word NIGGER *symbolizes almost four hundred years of anti-African racism and cultural repression.*

Geraldine L. Wilson
Bulletin (Council on
Interracial Books for Children),
Vol. 11, Nos. 3 & 4, 1980

Teenager Belinda VanKirk, whose family includes Chinese and Anglo/white ancestry, says she has often been called a "Chinese chicken" by classmates, but she has never felt it was a derogatory term—rather, she said, "it was a way for boys to flirt. And kids used to make it known that 'nobody could mess with Belinda 'cause she'll give you a karate chop!' I never straightened them out about karate being a Japanese thing! Anyway, I think it's great being kind of different. I've gotten a little more attention in school."

Sixteen-year-old Shanon, who appears more "white" than his neighbors in a predominantly white suburban area, says he fits well in his neighborhood school. He also feels at home in the industrial inner-city area that is primarily black, where many of his father's relatives live. "I go downtown to this boxing club with my cousin and every kind of color of kid is there. At first the guys called me 'oreo' and 'half-breed' and 'zebra.' They tried to get me mad. But I learned to take it. You have to if you want to be an amateur boxer. 'Cause people are going to yell at you, call you names when you're in the ring. Like the Mexican guys, they have to be cool when people in a crowd yell and call them 'taco benders' and 'greasers' and 'wetbacks.' If you let it get to you, you get rattled and lose a fight."

"In our school we had to put up with a lot of stuff from black kids for a while. They called us 'chocolate chip

*"I've often been called a 'Chinese
chicken' but that was a way for the
boys to flirt."—Belinda VanKirk, age 17.
(Belinda and her mother, Sandra)*

cookies' or 'high yellows' or 'white niggers'—junk like
that," sixteen-year-old June Carter said, speaking for her
biracial younger brothers as well as herself. "Sometimes
the black kids put us down because we have white
friends. There was a bunch used to talk about us, too.
Once it got back to me that a black guy in my class said
he saw me coming to school in the morning and that he
was asking everybody who that 'white bitch' was driving
me in the car. I could have jumped him, I was so mad.
That was my mama he was talkin' 'bout! Still, that's
really the worst kind of thing that's happened to us—
mostly bad-mouthing.

"All of us have found that it's better to just ignore and laugh at some of the dumb junk people say. Anyway, we've got both black and white friends now. I like to kid around a lot, but some of my black friends don't know how to take me. I told one black girlfriend she was in the oven too long. She got mad and said I wasn't in the oven long enough and I was no better than a white girl. We didn't talk to each other for about a week, but after that we were okay. That's just stuff girls do, you know, fight for a while and make up. It's no big thing."

June managed to handle name-calling with a sense of humor; Shanon rationalized racial slurs, making them a badge of acceptance in the boxing club; and Belinda saw her "name tag" as a status symbol. But it is not usually that easy to shrug off verbal attacks or to exhibit the kind of bravado expressed in the old saying, "Sticks and stones will break my bones but names will never hurt me." The truth is, *name-calling can hurt*. And those who resort to verbal abuse want to inflict pain and show their contempt and hostility for others.

"The pervasiveness of name-calling in our society facilitates and 'legitimizes' the use of racial name-calling and epithets," wrote Louise Derman-Sparks, in the *Bulletin*, published by the Council on Interracial Books for Children (CIBC). Ms. Derman-Sparks explained in a special issue on racism that "Name-callers use and/or seek the protection of the power of the society when they name-call."[5] In other words, people who name-call feel free to use this type of behavior to hurt others. Habitual name-callers seldom feel remorse or guilt in using racial slurs.

Kids who are able to deal with racial slurs usually have parents who early on have helped take the sting out of name-calling. As one Chicago teenager put it: "In grade school, I went home crying one day because somebody had called me a honky. I asked my mom if that's what I was and she told me, 'Some people will label you that and others will call you a nigger. But people call you names because it makes them feel superior. They have problems with their own self-worth. You're lucky—you know you're mixed and what a beautiful person you are.' "

According to thirteen-year-old Maria, whose father is of English background and whose mother is of Mexican heritage, it also helps when there are supportive adults at school to set the record straight. "Kids in my school used to get to me when they called me Mexican," Maria explained. "I wouldn't have any problem with being called Mexican—I *am* part Mexican and I *look* Mexican. But it's the *way* kids say it, like you're dirty or something. I felt a lot better when a teacher at school took my side and told the class about the good things Mexican people have going for them."

A teacher can play a major role in reeducating students and helping them to unlearn stereotypes. It is especially important for school personnel to deal constructively with name-calling situations when children are very young. For example, in Philadelphia, Pennsylvania, Tina Rafael says she and her husband, Don, will be "forever grateful" to their son's kindergarten teacher who "helped all the children in the class understand that name-calling is not appropriate behavior."

The situation began on the playground of an integrated school. Zackery, the son of a school counselor, knew that Elliot Rafael, with his blue-gray eyes, brown curly hair, and fair skin, was biracial. Elliot was also a small child, and so a likely candidate for someone intent on being the class "bully." As Tina explained it: "Zackery tormented Elliot for days, calling him a 'nigger.' I went to the principal about the problem. But I was told not to worry about it, that 'nigger' was just a word and that name-calling was just something kids did—I should ignore it. But then I asked the principal, who is Jewish, how he'd like it if some kid was calling his child a 'kike.' I mean, words aren't just words when they are used as weapons. But it took Elliot's teacher to point that out.

"One day after the tormenting had reduced Elliot to tears again, the teacher got up in front of the class, took Elliot by the hand, and told all the youngsters that she and Elliot were going to stand in the corner. 'All those in the class who want to use ugly names and call Elliot a 'nigger' will have to call me one, too,' the teacher announced. Of course, that demonstrated dramatically for the class that the teacher was supporting Elliot. She is so light-skinned (like Elliot) that I'm sure the youngsters didn't know she was biracial. But the point is, she showed she'd take the onslaughts with him. The name-calling stopped."

In a sequel to the story, Elliot went up to Zackery the next day, grabbed the larger boy around the waist and hugged Zackery so hard his feet left the floor. "What you need is some love, Zackery," Elliot said. Then, that same day, Elliot told Zackery's mother that she should spend more time with Zackery. "He just needs to be loved so he won't be so mean," Elliot declared.

"Out of the mouths of babes!" Tina laughed. "Naturally, I was proud of Elliot—we had often talked about each child needing his or her own special time with a parent. But I didn't realize how well he had absorbed the idea. And I was glad he was able to forgive and forget."

Sometimes, though, parents can be almost paranoid about possible insults and taunts that might be inflicted on their children. Judy, a white mother of a Mixed child living in Michigan, admits that when her son Adam was preschool age, she was "always on the defensive, just waiting to pounce on any kid in the neighborhood who might use racial slurs against Adam. I also wanted to make sure my son didn't learn that kind of behavior himself. I remember once Adam and his friend were playing with a little boy who's crippled—he scooted along on a skateboard-type platform because he'd lost his legs when a train ran over him. Whenever anyone was in his way, he'd say 'beep beep' and the other kids would scatter.

"One morning I heard Adam and his friend talking about the disabled boy, calling him 'weird,' and I thought this would be a good time for an object lesson about name-calling. So I started to get on the kids. But Adam's friend just looked at me like I was from outer space. And he said, 'We call that boy 'weird' because he says 'beep beep' all the time. But maybe he has to because people can't see him down so low.' I shut my mouth! Obviously, Adam and his friend were not ridiculing the other boy's physical difference—they in fact accepted the way he was. I learned something that day—not to be too quick to take offense!"

Yet, it is difficult not to be wary, especially if as a young person you have been the victim of racism and/or ethnic stereotyping. In some cases, that stereotyping can be in the form of expecting too much. For example, some biracial young people of Asian/white parents say they have been called "eggheads," and in school teachers have expected them to be brilliant in math, science, and similar technical subjects.

"People get the idea that just because you have Asian ancestry you are supposed to be some kind of scientific genius," said one girl of Japanese/white parentage. "I hate math and I'm a lousy science student. My thing is acting and dance. It bugs me, too, when clerks in stores talk to me in a loud voice and stilted Pidgen English, like I can't understand the language! Some people even ask me how long I've been in the United States. It's frustrating. I was born in Sacramento. I'm an American!"

A midwesterner of Chinese/white ancestry said that she can remember a few instances of kids trying to put her down with the "Chinaman chant" and being taunted with "Chink." But, she said, "for the most part the problems weren't so much with name-calling as with the attitude that white people have—they treat those who are different as if they don't know anything. And once some old guy who lived next door to us had the nerve to tell us kids that we ought to go back where we came from. I remember wondering if that meant Indiana was a foreign country, because that's where we had lived before moving to Illinois."

Christina, of German/Mexican parentage, who spent her teen years on a major university campus where her father is a music professor, also has had more problems with stereotypical attitudes than with name-calling. "It's like people expect you to enjoy all Mexican music when it comes on the radio," she said. "Or sometimes at school when we had tamales or tacos for lunch, kids would say, 'You must have these a lot at home,' or 'You must be used to all this hot food,' and I'd say, 'why? We eat a lot of different kinds of food.' It still bugs me when people assume we eat only Mexican foods because my mom is Mexican," Christina said. She added that the worst kind of stereotyping came not from classmates but from a teacher.

"She—the teacher—was presenting a social studies unit on Mexico and she told the class that the main food was tortillas and beans and that the culture was very poor. Well, that's just not true—I mean the entire country is not that way," Christina said. "But the teacher convinced the class it was, and she used the same approach when talking about other countries. She even brought in a roll of rough toilet paper, passed it around the classroom and told the kids to 'feel how hard it is.' She said that was the kind of poor quality product people in Jamaica used!"

Whatever the form of racism and ethnic stereotyping, there are coping methods that interracial and interethnic family members have found helpful. One is to teach offspring as much as possible about the positive aspects of their heritage. Another is to assure victims of name-calling that they are not at fault. Young children, who often personalize traumatic incidents, especially need to know that they are not responsible for racial slurs that come their way.[6]

Parents also believe it is important to point out to their children that many people "are carefully taught" to act in racist ways. Racist behavior may be learned in families, from friends, through messages and stereotypical portrayals of various cultural groups in the media (books, magazines, TV) and in schools and other institutions. But in no way can racist behavior be justified or name-calling condoned, say child guidance experts, even though there could be many reasons, including fear and ignorance, for racist actions.

"We feel we have to also explain to our children about socioeconomic differences," said a California doctor whose biracial children were victims of name-calling when they attended primarily black schools. "In such instances, we tried to explain that black kids might have been letting our biracial kids know that their lighter color and so-called white behavior and speech didn't make them better. Perhaps the black kids were trying to cut our kids down 'to size.' But wherever name-calling comes from, we feel that it must be discussed openly. In fact, race itself is a matter for family discussion because that's how we've helped our kids gain a positive identity, which is one of the best defense mechanisms against racial slurs."

This point was underscored by Amanda Houston-Hamilton, psychotherapist at the University of California, San Francisco. However, Dr. Houston-Hamilton pointed out that many parents in interracial families simply do not talk about race. Perhaps they are confused about what to say. Or they may be angry or anxious or want to ignore the subject, hoping to protect or shield their children. Some parents believe their children are "color-blind," since they do not talk about people in terms of race. Yet, many studies have shown that children at a very young age are aware of not only color differences but also internalize value judgments about race/color.

Because racial issues are not discussed, "young people who are biracial often tell me that they have never shared with other family members what it is like to be biracial and to be a person of color," Dr. Houston-Hamilton said. As a result, biracial children have to deal with cultural and social issues by themselves. "It is important to share with children that some of the race issues are just plain crazy and that trying to find some rational understanding about race is truly bizarre. Because it is *not* a rational issue—no matter how biologists try to explain race, there just is no explanation that makes sense. It's as if biologists sat down and said it was just too confusing to have all these different people, so they tried to divide up masses by types of hair and noses and so on and on. How can you explain something like that to a young child?" Dr. Houston-Hamilton asked, adding that "parents should explain that it is okay to muddle through things that are very confusing, and even though certain racial issues trouble us, we can still talk about them."

COMMUNITIES OF COLOR

4

The ideal society would enable
every man and woman to develop
along their individual lines, and
not attempt to force all into one
mould [sic], however admirable.

J.B.S. Haldane

lthough the Curtis family has had to put up with occasional racial slurs, they have experienced little of that type of harassment in Cass County, Michigan. "People in our area are used to mixtures. Lots of folks around here come from a long line of 'mixed bloods,'" said sixteen-year-old John Curtis. He had just come into the house after tending to the farm animals and was gettting ready to enjoy a Sunday afternoon football game on TV.

"Tell you the truth," John's father, Bob, said, "Our life is so common, I don't know what there is to talk about." Bob settled back in his easy chair as his wife, Joan, came in from the kitchen, where she'd been canning the last of the fruit harvest. "Out here, not much happens," she agreed, and gestured toward their large living-room window, which framed a peaceful fall scene outdoors.

Indeed, it was hard to imagine any type of disturbance other than the sounds of a tractor in the fields, or the cry of birds in formation on their way south, or crickets chirping in the garage as night began to close in. And in the warm atmosphere of the Curtis household, talk of any racial conflict or differences seemed out of place.

"There've never been any problems at school," John said, adding with a shrug: "People around here just do their own thing—they don't get into other people's business."

"We go to work, farm a little, see some family people, keep adding to the house and farm buildings . . . ," Bob broke in, then pointed out that he had built his home him-

"People in our area are used to mixtures."
—John Curtis, age 16. (John is shown with
his father, Bob Curtis, who is of Native American/
black/white ancestry, and his mother, Joan,
who comes from a Pennsylvania Mennonite
background; John Curtis considers himself Mixed.)

self on his portion of an eighty-acre (32-ha) farm. It was perched on a hill at the crossroads, one leading to Calvin Center, the other to Cassopolis, the county seat.

These villages, along with such small towns as Vandalia and Dowagiac and a resort area called Paradise Lake, are part of a unique biracial community that has existed for more than a century. A group of Quakers settled the area in the early 1800s. They had fled the South because of their distaste of and zealous opposition to slavery and the persecution they themselves suffered for their religious beliefs. The Quaker settlement quickly became one of the stations along the Underground Railroad, where fugitive slaves were harbored on their way to freedom in Canada. Later, the Quakers encouraged free people of color and exslaves to settle on the Michigan farmland.[7]

Although other communities in the United States may be able to boast long histories of harmonious race relations, the Cass County, Michigan, area has often been cited as one in which whites and blacks have lived in peace and in a spirit of cooperation since before the Civil War. Yet, residents do make distinctions in regard to race. Some categorize themselves as "white," while others call themselves "colored" or "Calvinites." Those who identify as Calvinites tend to be regarded as "light, bright, and damned-near white," according to one old-timer.

The Calvinites *are* the "old-timers" in the area, tracing their heritage back to the beginnings of the rural settlement. Many of their ancestors were of mixed parentage, descendants of white plantation owners and black slave women. Thus, the Calvinites today have inherited fair complexions and might appear to be "white." In the past, many chose to pass for white in order to get and keep good jobs and to be accepted in social situations outside the community.

Being identified as "white" or "near-white" has been a kind of status symbol over the decades, Bob Curtis said, explaining that over the years the coloreds in this area have discriminated against each other as much as blacks and whites in other places. "There are light-colored folks who don't want anything to do with dark ones, and have been that way for a long time." However, with the advent of black pride, light-complexioned "coloreds" have sometimes been seen as "uppity" and even as "traitors to their race."

Yet, many light-complexioned Calvinites would deny they have attitudes of superiority. Rather, they feel they cannot identify with either white or black. "We don't think of ourselves in racial terms," one woman said. "Our families have been here a long time, we live peacefully, have a good life, and we aren't out to make problems and trouble."

What about the "white folks," most of whom live in the small towns and in the county seat, Cassopolis? Are interracial families and people of color well accepted in the small towns? A white librarian made it clear before responding that she didn't believe in racial mixing but that she knew of a Mixed family which "lives up the street and they don't have any trouble at all." And a white construction worker noted that "I see lots of Mixed couples around here. Today, they come from the big cities, like Chicago and Detroit, and go to our bars and the lakes—you know, they just want to have a good time. I suspect a lot of them are just weekend affairs."

"Well, I can't say there's been a real welcome mat put out for Mixed families in town, not in Cassopolis, anyway," Bob Curtis said slowly. "I mean, it used to be a colored person wouldn't be hired in the bank or as a clerk in a store. And when I was a kid I wasn't allowed in the bowling alley. That's all changed since the sixties, but there definitely was some discrimination—mostly under-cover—where the white folks lived. It wasn't until 1964–65 that the village had a colored policeman—and I was the first to be appointed by the Chief. Then I broke some ice on the Village Council, got on it a few years later."

Out in the rural areas, though, life has gone on with-out much thought to color differences. About 80 percent of the forty thousand-plus residents of Cass County live on the farmlands. Approximately 10 percent of the county population is black (or "colored") and most live on their own farms in a four-township area that extends in each direction from the Curtis property.

"Shoot. This was my father's farm and he divided it up among his children and we've all built close by," Bob explained, adding that he was following a typical pattern among rural families. He also stressed that in his family "colored and white have always gotten along. Fact is, my mother's mother was white and her dad was colored, so my mother taught us that a person is a person no matter what."

That same type of upbringing was part of Joan's early life. She was raised in a Pennsylvania Mennonite community which she said was "very religious." Since there were no "colored people around at all, we didn't even discuss differences like black and white. The first black person I ever really saw was in a hospital where I went to work when I was nineteen. That sounds weird, I know. But I wasn't really color-conscious until then. I mean there were some kids who came to our community to get out of the city for a while. They were called 'fresh-air kids.' But I didn't realize until I got older and looked back and saw pictures of the kids that they were colored. It just never registered that the kids I played with had different skin color. So I didn't grow up with any of the prejudices that you had to stay away from someone because that person was black or from some other ethnic group. Even today, if a person comes to the door and Bob asks me if he or she was black or white, I can't honestly tell him unless I stop to think about it."

It hardly seems possible that a rural Michigan "community of color" would have anything in common with a Chicago neighborhood. But the Hyde Park area on the city's south side has long been a "community of color" and is home base for many interracial families. Most pick the Hyde Park neighborhood because, as one resident put it, "The area is the only successful integrated community in the city."

The neighborhood extends about ten blocks from north to south around the University of Chicago and from the edge of the campus on the west about ten blocks east to Lake Michigan. Because of the university, many residents are students, professors, and personnel working on the campus. People from all parts of the world are drawn to the area. In short, it is a kind of microcosm of the planet.

"I love being here," said one single mother who is biracial. "My son's father is black and yet my son, like me, is very fair-skinned and looks more Hispanic, so he's starting to ask questions about his color and who he is. I'll certainly talk to my son about sharing his father's heritage —his father no longer lives with us—but its hard for a five-year-old to understand, because he 'looks white.' So being in a community like Hyde Park, my son is around people who not only represent different races but also a variety of countries. It's truly a healthy environment for us."

Michael and Rosena Kruley agree with that assessment of their neighborhood. Michael, who is Jewish, and Rosena, who is black, say that it is a special advantage to be able to bring up their son and daughter where they will be around people like themselves—mixed youngsters in the parks, in the schools, at the shopping centers, and in the restaurants and food shops. "We think about moving because our family is outgrowing our apartment, but we feel we have to be very selective about any other place where we might live. Many other areas of the city and certainly many suburban communities would not be as receptive to our family," Michael said.

The Kruleys also belong to the Chicago Biracial Family Network, a group of interracial families that meets regularly in Hyde Park for social and recreational activities as well as for educational purposes. They feel the group has been helpful because of the supportive people, those who may have had similar experiences and can tell how they cope or deal with racist attitudes or discriminatory practices.

"But we don't feel we've had a lot of problems," Rosena was quick to point out. "We were aware of people staring when we first got married, especially when we were in the southwest [ethnic] neighborhoods and out in the white suburbs. But I think the more comfortable a couple is with themselves the less they are conscious of others' curiosity."

The "comfort factor," for want of a better term, is often the reason given for living in a "community of color" such as Hyde Park. "You don't have to think all the time about differences—you just accept them," said a black man who is an Air Force officer and interracially married. "I grew up in Hyde Park," he said, "and it was a natural thing to be around mixed families and biracial kids, so I didn't think it was unusual to marry a white woman. I also see a lot of Mixed kids coming into the cadet program that I command—we're stationed by Midway Airport. The white cadets often ask the Mixed kids how they can live with a white and black parent, like they think it's going to be freakish or something. The cadets who are Mixed say 'I don't look at my parents as black and white—they're Mom and Dad!' I mean—there's acceptance. That's the way it is! What I'm trying to say is that living in Hyde Park is something like that. The neighborhood is home for many interracial families and that's just the way it is!"

Interracial families living on or near military bases across the nation believe that these areas, too, are hospitable. "We live near the Air Force base at Colorado Springs and our black/white interracial family certainly is not unusual," explained one mother. "Everywhere we see Mixed families—Asian/black, Puerto Rican/white, Native American/white, Hispanic/white, Hispanic/black—there are a lot of mixtures."

Many Mixed families choose to live in neighborhoods around large universities and in cosmopolitan cities such as San Francisco and New York. However, a number of interracial adults say that living in a community of color may not be as important as how they present themselves—in positive, nondefensive ways. The economic and educational backgrounds of the people with whom family members associate are also factors in whether an interracial family is comfortable in a community. At least that is the opinion of John and Janine Brown of Atlanta, Georgia, who are Massachusetts transplants. John, who identifies himself as black, and Janine, who is white, have two biracial children and feel that there has been a more 'tolerant' attitude toward their family in Atlanta than in the Northeast.

"Of course, if you are working for or get involved some way with the 'good ol' boy' types, then you could have problems being part of an interracial family," John said. "But for the most part, economics seems to be a great equalizer here. Janine and I both work for AT&T and I would say we are middle-class. Our friends and associates are in about the same income bracket and are both black and white, plus we are involved with an interracial family support group. We just don't bother to deal with people—whether family or otherwise—who want to cause us aggravation."

Janine agrees, adding that some black/white interracial families segregate themselves in all-black communities or neighborhoods and get involved only in black activities. "I don't feel this is any more healthy for biracial children than being segregated in an all-white area. We have deliberately enrolled our two youngsters, Jeanetta and Jacob, in integrated day-care centers. John and I feel the kids need to relate with children who represent both sides of their heritage. So I guess in a sense they are in small 'communities of color.'"

A FAMILY AFFAIR

5

*If you marry him you aren't
welcome here! We don't
want you bringing any
Mixed grandchildren home!*

A parent

Being accepted in a community may be especially important to interracial and interethnic couples who have been rejected by parents, grandparents, or other relatives. Conflicts with extended family members are, in fact, some of the most difficult problems with which some interracial and interethnic families have to cope.

"Couples often think when they marry that they are the only two that matter—but I think that's a mistake. In many ways, you really marry the family, too," said Lanette, a young professional on the staff of a network radio station in Chicago. Lanette, who is black, married her husband, Phil, in the seventies. Phil, also with the radio station, is white. "Not Anglo," Phil was quick to emphasize. "I'm of Czech ancestry and our family is involved in a lot of Bohemian traditions—with food and customs."

"For a while after our marriage, Phil's parents didn't want any part of me," Lanette interjected. "They refused to come to our wedding. But most of the other relatives were there, including Phil's grandmother."

"She was the catalyst," Phil explained. "She helped bring about a change in my parents and took their place in our lives for a while. It really helps to have support and approval from family—with your family you expect to be your real self."

However, for more than a year Phil's parents kept their distance, even as other relatives rallied around the couple. Phil's parents gradually began to acknowledge and then finally accept their daughter-in-law. But Lanette has a

...fficult time forgetting some of her in-laws' objections, which ranged from "I don't want to walk the street with any black grandchildren" to "There must be something wrong with Phil if he couldn't find a nice white girl to marry."

As for Lanette's family, there was no animosity. An only child, Lanette attended a Catholic girls' school, which, she said, "was predominately black, but I was on the forensic and debate team, and we were in an inter-Catholic league, which meant that we went to meets with primarily white schools. So, I got used to competing and making friends in the so-called white world. In fact, there were always so many white folks around that the mother of my best friend on the block asked me, when I announced my engagement to Phil, if I was marrying somebody white. When I said 'yes,' my friend's mother said, 'I just figured you would!' It wasn't a put-down—just a kind of natural assumption."

As Phil's parents began to include Lanette within their family circle, the couple could relax and enjoy holiday celebrations, reunions, and the like with Phil's relatives. "We were patient and, as the saying goes, time seemed to heal the rift between us," Phil said.

"We talked about all of this long before we got married," Lanette added. "I think that's very important—before any marriage, there should be lots of discussion about possible conflicts, whether it's family disapproval or differences in food preferences or how traditions should be observed."

By discussing differences, two people can learn to respect and understand each other's culture, said another midwestern couple, Rod and Sue, who also were married in the seventies. While still in college, where they met, they frankly discussed family patterns as possible sources of friction. Sue reported that her mother, a nurse, and father, an agricultural teacher and farmer, were concerned about what the neighbors would think if they saw their daughter dating a black man.

"Mother was particularly anxious, constantly asking 'What about us? Don't you know what you're doing to your father and me?' I'm sure she felt these were legitimate concerns—she had never questioned the basis of her attitude. She just accepted all the racial stereotypes many whites have learned—she never tried to relate to someone of a different color or ethnic background on an individual basis," Sue said, adding that "Rod and I went on with our plans to marry and never pushed for acceptance —we just let my folks come to us, which they did right after we were married. They became very supportive, especially after their first grandchild was born!"

Rod's family in Panama was not particularly concerned about Sue's Anglo ancestry, that is, they were not adamant that Rod marry someone of his own race. Rather, Rod's father, a retired military officer, had advised his son to marry a Panamanian only because life would be easier. "An Anglo wife might not understand how Panamanian families function," his father said.

"My people expect anyone in the family who has 'made it' (financially speaking) to send money or other gifts back home," Rod explained. "When they come to visit, they expect us to pay for everything, will even demand that. And I'm expected to pay for my younger sister's college education."

"I wasn't too keen about any of this at first," Sue said. "It was so opposite to U.S. family life. Usually parents are helping kids get settled. Now, though, I see it as a sort of family Red Cross. We share where it is needed among our own."

Although many couples work out their family differences, sometimes there is no way to break down rigid barriers set up by racist attitudes. Some parents and other relatives of black/white interracial couples absolutely refuse to accept in-laws or even grandchildren. Outright rejection most often comes from whites.

"About half the black/white interracial families I've met in the Washington, D.C., area where we live have experienced rejection from white family members," reported Lynne Bobbitt, who is white and whose husband, Joe, is black. However, Lynne added, many families reconcile in time, especially when grandparents see their grandchildren and learn to know them. But that has not been possible for the Bobbitts.

The couple and their two young children, Danny and Janelle, live in Lothian, which Lynne describes as "totally white" and known for its excellent school system—the main reason the Bobbitts chose the community for their home. "My family has lived close by—just 13 miles (21 km) from us—for nearly nine years, ever since Joe and I have been married, but we have been almost completely cut off. My father refuses to see or even acknowledge the children," Lynne said. "I sent him pictures of the children, but he asked me not to send any more. When the kids ask me about my father, I have to tell them that he won't visit because he doesn't like their father—he doesn't like black people—which is his loss. When the children get older I hope I can point out how contradictory my father's view is. My father is part Native American and I've tried to find out why he objected to our interracial family when he is obviously Mixed. But he would never discuss the matter."

Julie, who is white and grew up in Des Moines, Iowa, has had a similar experience with parental rejection. During the sixties, Julie moved to California, where she married a black man. Their two boys are now adolescents. When their oldest son was five, "he wanted to know why grandpa wouldn't come from Iowa to visit when grandma did." Julie explained that her father had expected her to marry a white man and was very disappointed because she had not. "I told my son that my dad had always been around white people and that grandpa is a man who is very frightened of people who are different. He doesn't know that it's a lot of fun to be around many different kinds of people. And if he came to visit he wouldn't be very nice to you." After trying to absorb the meaning of his mother's explanation, Julie's son looked at her with a puzzled expression and said: "But I'm only five. How can grandpa be scared of me?"

Of course there is no satisfactory answer to such a question. And as one parent said: "There is no way to make such a situation 'right.'" But some parents help their young children deal with such rejection by pointing out that it is not personal. Rather, when a family member rejects another because of racial or ethnic differences, that family member suffers from a sickness brought on by a racist society.

Another important coping method that parents use in family rejection situations is to simply show their children that life goes on. Children need to see that their parents can continue with their day-to-day living and are not devastated by ostracism. "You don't have to like it or be a martyr about it," said Barbara, a white mother of two biracial children. "But when parents would rather see you dead than have anything to do with you, you have to be strong within your interracial family."

Barbara hasn't seen her father for years because "as soon as he found out I was living with a black man, he went berserk," she said. "He got out a shotgun and went storming out the door, threatening to kill me and Joe and anyone around us. And he blamed my mother, saying she raised me wrong!"

Barbara explained that her parents live in Michigan's Upper Peninsula and that her mother finally did come to their suburban Detroit home to visit a few times, bringing gifts for her grandchildren. "My mom told me that she thought Dad was beginning to come around since he had a hunting buddy who is black and married to a white woman. But Dad told Mom that if I come to see them I have to leave the *monkeys* behind! I wouldn't call that acceptance!"

"They just can't help it," Joe said, shrugging. "They used to live in Klan country in southern Indiana. I've learned to ignore such 'redneck' types. We ignore the other bigots, too—the ones that yell 'nigger lover' at Barbara or ask her why she doesn't get a 'real black one' while she's at it. You have to stay away from people like that or you get really strung out. We don't mess with black street people either—the ones who like to agitate by calling my sons 'yellow niggers.' Racism is racism no matter where it comes from."

Bill, an Indiana businessman who is black and married to a white woman, agrees. "We went to visit my parents in Mississippi after we were married and one of my sisters came over and really made a scene," Bill said. "This sister has been into 'being black' since the seventies and she's just consumed with hate for white people. She tried to force my wife out of my parents' home. Since that time I haven't had much to do with that sister."

Sharon, a teacher who is white and married to a black man who is an electrician, faced a similar situation. "When Charles and I got married his two older sisters came over to let us know that they were 'violently opposed' to our marriage, although I didn't feel hostility from the rest of Charles's family. Now, two years after our marriage, we go to family gatherings and nobody gets on our case. I think Charles's sisters were really trying to protect him— I mean he was over thirty when we got married—it was a first marriage for him and a second for me."

Of course not all interracial couples have to face family disapproval. Ae Ja, who is Korean, and John, who is of Anglo/white heritage, cannot recall any outward prejudice or discrimination toward their interracial family. They live with their daughter, Christina Lee, and Ae Ja's mother in a conservative industrial town in the Midwest. The two met by correspondence while Ae Ja was in Korea and John in the United States.

For more than a year, the two wrote letters to each other, exchanged photos, and developed a "paper relationship." Then John proposed via correspondence. Ae Ja accepted, but conditionally—John had to be approved by her family.

"When John came to Korea everybody looked him over, and my family and friends thought he would fit in fine because he is short like us," Ae Ja said with a quick smile. But a more important factor in acceptance was being able to communicate with family members. John does not speak Korean but can converse fluently in Japanese, a second language in Korea. This impressed Ae Ja's family because he was able to carry on conversations with them. Even today, Japanese is the language he uses to converse with his mother-in-law, who has come to live in his home.

"When Ae Ja first came to the United States, she was very homesick," John said. "The Korean culture is family-oriented; that is, the whole society is based on family relationships—who's related to whom. Ae Ja knows every one of her extended family members back several generations. Then, when we got married and she left her country, it was really a cultural shock."

"Yes, but John's parents were very supportive," Ae Ja interjected. "I really appreciate my mother-in-law—she is like my mom. And the rest of John's family have been the best. Without them I don't think I would have made it. I was crying all the time because I felt so—so—strange. I had to learn how to drive, to speak the language better —I had learned a little English in Korea. But I felt like I was in a body case—a box. I began to wonder if I'd made a mistake getting married, and I didn't want to think about having my own family.

"After about two years or so, though, I began to adjust. And of course we have our Christina—Christy, we call her

"Christy sometimes tells us she is Korean, and she looks a little like our people. But her eyes are blue and her hair brown! She inherited that from John's side."—Ae Ja, Christy's mother. (Four generations pose: in front are John and Ae Ja Chapman; in the back are John's mother, Christy, John's grandmother, and Ae Ja's mother.)

—and my mother is here now from Korea to help. I'm hoping to go to work soon and my mom baby-sits while I go to cosmetology school."

Ae Ja explained that Christina has learned to speak both Korean and English, changing as necessary to talk with her Korean grandmother and American grandparents and family. "Christy sometimes tells us she is Korean, and she looks a little like our people. But her eyes are blue and her hair brown! She inherited that from John's side."

John added that he thought Christy would have some special advantages being biracial. "We expect she will appreciate both American and Korean cultures as she grows up."

Being able to appreciate two different cultures is also an important aspect in the development of a healthy self-concept for children who have part-Hispanic heritage. But like many other ethnic or racial groups, there is no monolithic Hispanic culture or community. Hispanic is an "umbrella term" for many different Spanish-speaking peoples and a variety of heritages. In addition, some Spanish-speaking people have been part of the English-speaking American culture for several generations, while others may be new arrivals to the United States.

Within many Hispanic families, though, parents often express similar fears about their children marrying outside their particular culture. One common concern is that children will face ridicule or put-downs if they use the Spanish language or take part in various festivals and follow national customs. Yet, as with other intermarriages, language and custom differences are not necessarily barriers to successful unions—if each spouse respects the other's heritage. That respect is then usually passed on to the children.

Louis Calo, who is Puerto Rican, and his wife, Jean, who is black, feel it is "just a natural thing" to teach their three mixed children to appreciate their dual heritage. The Calos make their home in Gary, Indiana, where they are often in touch with Jean's parents and relatives. But Louis's brother and his family also are close by and the Calos travel often to San Juan, Puerto Rico, where Louis's parents and many relatives live.

"We talk straight out to our kids about who they are," Jean said. "Angela, the oldest, is just six, but she has been asking questions for a long time about color. She couldn't understand why people called me black. 'You're brown,' she'd say. Because she has light skin like her daddy, she

Louis and Jean Calo want their children to know that their family has brought two cultures together—Puerto Rican and black.

thought she was white for a while. When I was carrying Robyn, who's a year old now, Angela kept asking if the baby was going to be white like her or black like me. She said she didn't want to have any black baby around— somehow I guess she'd already picked up the idea that being black wasn't such a good thing because of how people treat blacks. Anyway, we had to work with her and tell her that God made people of all different colors and skin color doesn't make the person."

"We had to straighten her out, too, when she'd come home from staying overnight with one of her white girl-friends," Louis said. "She'd correct our English, and put up her nose about eating neck bones and greens or eating rice and beans. We had to let her know right away that there is nothing wrong with the way we eat or speak or how our family lives."

Louis pointed out that they want their children to know that their family has brought two cultures together. "If my son, Louis, Jr., decides later on to call himself a black person, then that's his decision, but I'll be explaining all along that he isn't just black because then that says he's not part of me. He's Puerto Rican and black—mixed."

The Calos believe it will be helpful as their children grow up to live as they do in an integrated neighborhood. "We have mostly mixed friends, too—families that are black/white, Puerto Rican/white, Mexican/black—so I think the kids will just naturally learn that mixtures are okay," Jean said.

Growing up with people of many different colors and ethnic backgrounds is a definite advantage for anyone who is involved in an interracial family. At least that is how Joan Broadfield of Chester, Pennsylvania, sees it.

"Growing up with people of many different colors and ethnic backgrounds is a definite advantage for anyone who is involved in an interracial family." —Joan Broadfield. (Shown here are Ed and Joan Broadfield at their daughter Lara's graduation.)

Joan, who is white, says, "When I was a teenager my parents taught at a predominately black college, and we lived on the campus. I found myself in social situations with blacks more than with whites. My father is an anthropologist, and my parents had many friends who had married crossculturally or interracially. So it certainly was not considered unusual for me to date interracially or to marry a black man. Perhaps the only concern my parents had was that my life might be 'much harder,' as they put it. But I can honestly say that life has not been difficult—maybe that is because we are fairly well-established in our community—people know us," Joan explained.

Although Angela, who is white, and Walter Blythe, who is black, were not raised in integrated environments, they both learned at an early age to accept people on an individual basis. As Angela explained: "My parents taught me not to judge people by color or religion. When I was a kid our family lived in Salt Lake City for a while. And we found out what it was like to be discriminated against because we were not Mormon. Perhaps that's why my parents tried so hard to teach us that our white skin was not a mark of superiority. People are people no matter what their color or religious differences."

Now living in the Colorado Springs area, Angela says her extended family includes six black/white biracial children, two of whom are hers and Walter's. Angela's three sisters are also interracially married and live with their families nearby—a colorful rainbow when they all get together.

"Once an aunt asked my mother if she didn't long to have a blue-eyed, blond, or light-skinned, redheaded grandchild," Angela said, "but Mom just laughed and said 'No, because my grandchildren don't have to lie in the sun and expose themselves to skin cancer in order to get tan!'"

In a more serious vein, Angela pointed out that biracial children may have special advantages. "Of course

I'm biased," she said, "but I would really be interested in finding out more about the inherited traits of our children. Our doctor firmly believes that, biologically, biracial children reflect the best of both races."

"Let's face it," said an Atlanta mother of biracial youngsters, "we [interracial couples] produce beautiful children!"

"Not only that, mixed kids are much more mature than most of their peers," says Ben Barnes, a youth worker in Indiana who, for sixteen years, has been involved with many biracial young people in sports and social activities.

Chicagoans Ouida Lindsey, a newspaper columnist, and her husband Paul, a sociologist, pointed out in their book *Breaking the Bonds of Racism* that "Crocodile tears need not be shed" for the supposed psychic turmoil of children of mixed color heritage. As parents of biracial children, the Lindseys (she's black, he's white) had some straightforward advice for those who argue against interracial marriages because they think the children will suffer. "Since you see this [interracial marriage] as a problem for children you should make sure that you yourself act decently and supportively toward such children and counsel others to do likewise. . . ."

"THE DATING GAME"

6

When I first started dating Joe,
he sometimes had a hard time in
our neighborhood. Black guys
messed up his car and tried to
intimidate 'whitey' on the street.

A young black woman in Chicago

Interracial families may cope well with less-than-cordial relatives, they may be able to intelligently handle name-calling and other forms of bigotry and prejudice. But what happens when teenagers in the family begin to socialize? Do biracial young people have problems making friends? Is "getting a date" any more difficult for mixed kids than other teenagers? How do biracial single adults feel about "the dating game?"

Such questions are often raised in discussions about interracial families. Some observers believe biracial young people will face constant rejection—will be excluded from both a minority group and the dominant white group. Others believe biracial young people can pick and choose friends and dating partners from almost any cultural group. Like other issues surrounding "the rainbow effect," there is little concrete evidence to indicate whether socializing is any more difficult for interracial young people than for others in the society.

According to Dr. Poussaint's 1983 study of black/white biracial young adults (many of whom were attending Harvard), dating patterns were too varied to draw any firm conclusions. Some biracial adults who were light-skinned dated primarily whites. Others who were darker-skinned seemed to prefer dating blacks. Still, many dated on both sides.[8]

Of the forty-five biracial young people interviewed for this book, all but two reported that they felt comfortable being with people of nearly all cultures and colors. Most picked friends and dating partners not by color or ethnic background but by shared interests. As a number of teenagers said: "Color is no big thing when it comes to being with people you like. We aren't into racial stuff like the older generation. Black kids, brown kids, tan kids, white kids go together."

In Long Beach, California, Stacy Collins, a black/white biracial teenager, said "I usually pick my friends by their personalities and they seem to like me for the way I am. I try to make people feel good about themselves," she said, adding that maybe that was why she wanted to be a psychologist someday.

Young people with interracial heritage also expressed a kind of "one world" view and some felt they could become "whoever they were with." They appreciated differences and understood commonalities, a concept that has no doubt developed because of their interracial family structures and their parents' pride in their own identities.

Many biracial young people say that bigoted talk about ethnic groups can drive them "up the wall" or really rankle them. "Blacks might start talking about whites and whites might make remarks about blacks, or both groups might get on the Jews or Indians or Asians or Arabs or whatever. I think it's stupid—and I don't like all the dumb ethnic jokes, either," said a suburban Chicagoan whose heritage includes Polish and West Indian.

Dr. Houston-Hamilton has found in her many interviews with interracial families that biracial offspring have a sense of fairness and are not judgmental. One biracial child saw those who have values and views different from her family's as "just being on another team." And a biracial young adult described his attitude to Dr. Houston-Hamilton this way: "I never see things just as they seem, because I'm not [just as I seem]. So I assume that nothing is as it appears." In essence, the psychotherapist noted, people of mixed heritage are "harmonizers."[9]

However, no matter how much biracial young people may hope to "harmonize," they may experience difficulties in friendships and dating because of "outside" pressures—the prejudicial attitudes and underlying racism that permeate our society. And white rejection may be all too familiar to some biracial young people, especially if they are categorized by whites as being "black."

Jonathan, whose mother is white and father is black, reported a fairly typical experience. He attends a small Quaker high school in Pennsylvania, and explained that he had been seeing a white girl, but that "her mother is prejudiced, and so she wouldn't let me come to the house or talk to her daughter or anything. She just doesn't want me around at all," he said sadly.

This was not the first time Jonathan had encountered people who hurt his feelings because they could not accept his color and biracial heritage. But the experience will not be easy to forget, even though he says he realizes that others have problems and it is up to him to put a distance between prejudiced people and himself. Nevertheless, as Jonathan said, "It hurts."

Cathleen, a young woman of Mexican/Anglo background, reported a similar experience. Cathleen lives in southern California and recently broke off with a steady boyfriend because his family did not like the fact that one of her parents was Mexican. "It's a nasty story, really. One of my boyfriend's brothers didn't realize I was part Mexican—I guess my skin and hair weren't dark enough or something. Anyway, this guy was telling jokes about Mexicans and using terms like 'spics' and talking about greasy hair—the usual stereotypes and put-downs. Then I told him I didn't appreciate that kind of talk because I was part Mexican. He looked at me and said 'That's impossible—you aren't that stupid!' Well, I was really crushed. I found out most of my boyfriend's family had the same attitude. So I quit the relationship."

A young woman of Puerto Rican/white ancestry, teaching in a small town in Illinois, also broke off a relationship because of the prejudicial attitudes of her boyfriend's family. As she explained: "I'd met this fellow —another teacher—in the same school where I teach. We dated for quite a while and things were getting pretty serious. But when I'd go over to visit with his family, who are Italian, his parents would always ask me about my background. I had told them that I was part Puerto Rican, but they kept asking if I was Italian, since my skin color was kind of 'olive,' as they say. It was clear that being Italian would make it okay for me to date their son but that being Puerto Rican or Hispanic was not okay. Even the way they said 'Hispanic' made me feel it was a dirty word. It was the first time I'd really been forced to defend myself and say 'Hey, I'm proud of my heritage.' Anyway, the relationship between the other teacher and me cooled after that. I've decided to look for employment in another town, a place where there is more diversity and people from a variety of cultural and racial backgrounds."

Within most ethnic groups there are often family pressures on teenagers and young adults to socialize with "one's own kind." Four psychotherapists, George Kitahara Kich, Mary Ann Leff, Grace Wakamatsu Fleming, and Steve Shigematsu-Murphy, prepared a paper dealing, in part, with this subject. Presenting their views at a conference on Japanese-American Studies held at the University of California, Santa Cruz, in August 1985, the therapists explained that "outmarriage" in the Japanese-American community has been estimated to be from 50 to 70 percent. This has raised fears in the community, which has a strong sense of ethnic and cultural pride, that there will be a loss of Japanese cultural identity, especially if the children of interracial marriages do not carry on traditions, observe festivals, or respect other Japanese customs.[10]

Perhaps the fear of losing ethnicity is well-founded. Don Good, an Illinois man whose mother is Japanese and father is of German ancestry, said he knows very little about Japanese culture because his mother seldom talked

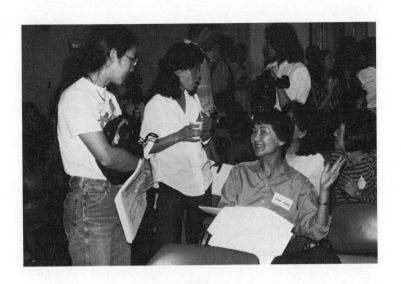

*Within some ethnic groups there
are family pressures to socialize
with "one's own kind."*

about it. Besides, he explained, "My father was a 'career'
Army man and we traveled a lot—around the United
States and to several different countries. As a result, I
don't think I actually put a lot of emphasis on my Japanese
heritage. When I started going out with girls I don't think
my 'mixed' race was ever brought up, although I obviously have some Asian features. If I had problems it was
because of my personality. I was always kind of with-
drawn, which I think came about because we moved so
much."

Obviously, no one experience represents how offspring
of interracial families handle social situations. But while
a good many biracial teenagers and young adults felt they
have a "free choice" in whom they will choose as friends
and dating partners, developing a serious relationship may
be another matter. One vivacious girl of black/white
heritage put it this way: "If you go after a white guy and

some other girl is after him too, you're told to cool it; but if you go after a black guy and another girl is interested in him, then nobody seems to care if you try to get to him. So it's sorta like the white guy has some special place and the black guy is nobody in particular, you know?"

"It's okay for any kid to go with someone of a different race," said another teenager. "But if, say, a white guy is a basketball or football star, then people might get upset if the guy goes with a Mixed or black girl. Just an ordinary white guy like me talks to black girls, nobody gets upset."

"Sometimes you hear guys talk, too, when they see white girls going with black guys—the girls are called 'nigger lovers' and some people think they're low-life," a 17-year-old biracial student in a large integrated school explained. "Nobody says that to me because they know I'm Mixed, but I hear the talk. It makes me mad."

Once more, as with other issues relating to interracial families, the "dating game" seems to create the most social disapproval when someone who is biracial is labeled "black" and dates a white person. Although other cultural or color combinations may create family problems, they do not result in as much public scorn. Yet, black/white biracial young people themselves do not appear to have personal conflicts regarding dating partners.

A fifteen-year-old of black/white parentage who lives in the Washington, D.C., area says he feels he can "date anyone of any race and I figure I'll deal with prejudice and hurt feelings if or when they come up. I don't worry about that now."

On the campus of Indiana University at Bloomington, in the midsection of the country, a young man in his twenties who is black/white biracial said: "I try to accentuate the positive in relationships. But I don't try to eliminate the negative—I'm always aware that an opposite force can be working. In other words, I don't expect people to destroy me, but I think I'm prepared to handle it if people don't want to be around me because of some prejudice. So that's the way I approach women I date. If I ever get into a serious relationship like marriage or living with someone, the woman would have to share such views."

Another single adult, Ramona Douglass, a sales representative in Chicago, has a similar opinion in regard to a "serious relationship" or a prospective marriage partner. "As a biracial I'd have to have a mate who is willing to take on the baggage that this society lays on people of color," she said. "So far I've not come across such a person yet. I've dated men of different races and cultures. Some time ago I was engaged to a Jewish man—I grew up in a predominately Jewish neighborhood in New York—but his mother said she would disown him if we married. He was kicked out of the house and that really crushed him, so we broke up. All his mother could perceive was my blackness, when in fact I am the product of an Italian mother and a father who is of Sioux Indian and black heritage," Ramona said.

She added that while growing up she related more to her mother's family and perhaps "felt more Italian" than black—"I was just never around any of my father's people —they lived in Colorado," she explained. "But I went through a period when I really wanted to get in touch with my black side—that was my identity crisis, I guess. Still, my father taught me that I had to *define myself*. Others might perceive me in a variety of ways. No matter how light my skin, most blacks will see me as black because of my black heritage. Some whites may think I'm Puerto Rican or of some other Hispanic group."

Ramona feels that "as a mixed person I have a perspective that many other people do not. My parents gave us a feeling of being special—not better—but a special knowing that something terrible does not happen when races mix; we're born—we're nice people—we very often have insights that people who are part of a single ethnic group may not have because they've kept themselves so separate. I think that's a gift that interracial parents give to their children. We incorporate both their cultures."

However, Ramona pointed out that her special perspective does not necessarily make it easier to find positive relationships with men. The dating game still is affected by how those of the opposite sex perceive her. "Black men often feel I'm intimidating—or at least that's the aura I give off, they say. And some Caucasians I've dated are on a fantasy trip about being with a woman they think is more sexually attractive because she's seen as black."

To sum up her experiences, Ramona believes that no matter how open and accepting a biracial person is of others, there is "always the reality out there—when push comes to shove, color will matter" in a serious relationship if the person of color is defined as unworthy or of lower status than the partner who is defined as one of the majority. "Such attitudes, unfortunately, still muck up the waters in human relationships," she said.

DIVORCE & REMARRIAGE

7

*Once my stepdad came to my classroom
and nobody knew what he was doing
there because there were no Asian kids
in the class. All heads turned and
some of the kids were whispering,
trying to figure out whose father he
might be. Then when they found out,
they came up to me and said, "Wow,
was that your father?" and I said
"Yes, doesn't he look like me?"
It does get funny sometimes.*

Anglo teenager talking
about her
Japanese-American stepfather

I admit it—I couldn't handle the pressure from my family and friends and at the last minute I backed out," said a young Jewish woman who had been engaged to a black man while both were on a college campus.

"I had the feeling my partner thought he had really done something—lifted me up—and that I should be grateful," a black woman said of her former live-in mate. "When I wanted to go back to school, he'd throw up comments like that, so I decided to split. I didn't want to depend on him."

"I couldn't cope with his family always telling us what to do and feeling like I was less important to him than his family," said an Anglo woman separated from her Hispanic husband. "One of his sisters still checks on me, comes over on the pretense that she's just making a friendly call. But I'm sure she talks about me."

"My family really loved Ron—he'd do anything for them," said a mother of Mexican ancestry with two biracial children. "But as a couple we couldn't get along—it had nothing to do with Ron being black. I think he's immature —not ready to take on the responsibilities of a family yet."

The causes for breakups expressed in the statements above are not all that different from those that might be described by any couple unable to overcome conflicts or live up to certain expectations in a relationship. The fact that some couples who split are identified as *interracial* leads many observers to conclude that color and/or cultural differences are barriers to harmony. Certainly religious differences, pressures from family and friends who disapprove, and job and housing difficulties related to discrimination *can* create friction. And conflicts might also arise in an interracial/interethnic marriage (as in any other) if there are major differences in the educational and occupational backgrounds of the spouses. Couples might then blame problems on racial/cultural factors.

However, when couples are compatible, share similar interests and are also mature enough to handle outside pressures, interracial or interethnic unions appear to be as strong, if not stronger, than those of people who marry within "their own group." As one interracial couple pointed out: "We think we work harder than most people do at maintaining a constructive relationship and developing a healthy and positive family life."

There is not enough case material to prove conclusively whether racial or cultural matters are at issue when interracial families split. But there is little doubt that separation and divorce can have a devastating effect on children—not because they are biracial but because the breakup of *any* family has the most severe impact on the children.

Hundreds of books and magazine articles plus newspaper features have been written on the problems common to children of divorce and separation and to children living in "remade," or "step"-families. The subject cannot be covered in any detail here. But interracial children whose families split and their custodial parents—usually mothers—may have to deal with "special" problems— that is, problems not usually encountered by the majority of divorced parents.

One of the problematic factors is the change in social status for a custodial parent and child because of loss of income. Dr. Janet Faulkner, who counsels many divorcing and single parents in the San Francisco Bay area, noted that white mothers with black/white children most often lose status, particularly if they have been reared in middle-class or affluent families. A white mother may have to move to a lower income area. She may also become more vulnerable, for the first time having to deal with overt acts of racism such as insulting remarks by strangers in the street and housing discrimination.

Dr. Faulkner added that "many white mothers who move into predominately black neighborhoods also have to learn how to handle comments by older black women who feel free to come up and tell them how to care for and discipline their children." Being corrected in public can be hard on a mother's ego and can make a mother feel she is inadequate when it comes to raising a biracial child. But, says Dr. Faulkner, "We must try to bury the myth that single white women can't raise black/white, Asian/white—or whatever, kids. We can't continue to lay that trip on mothers when so many other issues need to be considered."[11]

Another problematic factor for single mothers is the acute isolation and lack of supportive relatives. Some interracial families have already been cut off from extended family members, so after separation or divorce, the loss of family ties may be more keenly felt. A separated or divorced parent might also harbor resentment or hatred for a former spouse who is of another race or culture. This in turn could send negative messages to biracial children about one part of their heritage.

A black divorced mother from Brooklyn said she is trying to work out her animosity toward her former husband of ten years, who is Jewish. "I think a lot of my bitterness comes from the fact that his family never accepted me—I was always the 'nigger.' I know I have to straighten out a lot of my negative feelings because I don't want them to carry over to my daughter. She's just a baby now and I think of her as a totally black child and she's everything to me. I was in a store and there were two older black women behind me in the checkout line and the women looked at my daughter and said, 'Oh, she looks so white,' which made me upset. I guess I felt ashamed of her being part white. Like I say, I realize I have to work out this stuff—and I don't want my daughter to have to carry this."

A white divorced mother of two black/white biracial teenage sons said she also struggles with her feelings about the "ethnicity" of her children. She says she had a good marriage "which we outgrew" and feels no real resentment now toward her former black husband. But she admits that it sometimes upsets her to see her sons "being black," especially in speech patterns, and wonders if she is indeed carrying some kind of prejudicial attitudes about "blackness" because of her divorce. She, too, worries that she may pass some type of prejudice on to her children.

Concern about negatively influencing biracial children in regard to one side of their heritage seems to surface frequently in interracial families after parents split up. Dr. Faulkner and others who work with interracial families explain that separated parents may not have dealt with their own prejudices that could be destructive to their children's sense of self-worth. Racist attitudes can emerge, then, during divorce proceedings or in conflicts over visitation rights and in other matters regarding the care of biracial children.

Sometimes traumas are created for biracial children because of the so-called racial matching perpetuated by the court system. When a black/white interracial couple split, for example, a judge might decide that a child who "looks black" ought to be with the black parent.

Demetra Fountaine, a biracial adult born in the Chicago suburb of Glencoe, but now living in northern California, knows from her own experience some of the effects of such court decisions. Demetra's Greek mother and black father divorced when she was just a toddler.

Because her mother had to look for a job, Demetra and her younger sister were cared for by her father's parents. "After a year or so we all had to go to court because my mom had remarried (a white man) and wanted us back. But my father's family refused to give us up," Demetra said.

"I remember being in court and that my father's people cut my waist-length hair before we went, greased it, and did all they could to make me look blacker. They were awarded custody of my sister and me. The judge thought we should live with the black side of our family because we 'looked black,' or 'colored,' as they said then. The strange thing about this was that my black grandparents and their family lived in an all-white suburb and we went to an all-white school and my father married a white woman who became my stepmother. My mom and stepfather are white but they lived in an interracial neighborhood and had a number of interracial friends. This all became very contradictory and confusing to me at such a young age, and I started wishing I was white and hating the black part of me. I'd stare in the mirror and dream that my nose was small and pointed, and I'd admire my thin little lips and arched feet and thank God that I didn't have big lips and flat feet like my black relatives did."

Demetra explained that she became quite introverted and lonely because she wanted to "escape from the painful real world. I loved school when we lived in Glencoe because the teachers taught well and wanted the students to learn. Things changed dramatically when my sister and I went to live with my father and stepmother in an all-black, mainly poor, inner-city area. Then quite abruptly we moved to California. I found out much later that my mother had tried to regain custody, but my father didn't want her to have us, so he left Chicago without letting her know. My sister and I didn't see our mother for years and that created a deep longing and added to the psycho-

99

logical problems that built up because of being shifted from one family to another."

Demetra eventually was reunited with her mother and lived with her during her teen years. During that time she realized she had wanted to "be white" in order to be like her mother and live with her. But she vacillated, from the adolescent years through her twenties, trying to decide who she should be—biracial or black, living through the "black is beautiful" phase of American history, and now "being black," but knowing that "I *am* a mixture of black and white."[12]

Racial matching was also a primary factor in a custody case in Indiana, involving a divorced white mother, Myrna, with two white children. Myrna's problems began when she remarried. Her second husband is black.

Myrna had custody of her two children, Aaron and Angie, but the children's father "did not want to pay support, so he tried to use the fact that I was with a black man as a reason to take the children away from me," Myrna said. "When we went to court, my first husband's lawyer constantly raised racist questions. Like he asked, 'What about this colored guy? What if a white boy wants to date or marry your daughter and his parents won't let him because of the colored stepfather?' It was absurd. But stuff like that was put in the record. It was clearly discriminatory, but they figured they could get away with it because public opinion was on their side. The majority view in this part of the state is that it's degrading to have a black stepfather. My former husband thought I'd never appeal the case, because of the cost and hassle. But fortunately, I found a lawyer who was willing to carry the case as far as he could as a matter of principle. So the suit was dropped."

Clifford, Myrna's husband, said he "used to try to be civil with the children's father because I wanted the kids to respect him and I thought he ought to keep up his relationship with them, but he just went too far."

*Single moms and their kids:
Suzette and Chantel;
Ann and Sabrina*

Kay and Sarai

"That's putting it mildly," Myrna said. "What's so bad is he went for two years without ever visiting his children and I had to take them to their grandmother's so their father could at least see them. But the worst part is he used to preach to me all the time about being fair to people and he'd go on and on about how black people had been unjustly treated and should have equal opportunities. Since this custody thing, my son has sometimes come back from a visit with his father filled with anger and hatred."

"I don't know what his father tried to put in his head," Clifford said sadly. "Aaron would come home to us and tear up all the black things he could find—even tore off tires on his play trucks—and told me 'black was bad!' But things are getting better—we've been working with him."

It was a matter of undoing all the negatives, Myrna explained, and she feels progress has been made. Evidence of that progress, she said, revealed itself on a school exam her son was given on the subject of image: "The teacher was trying to find out how kids saw themselves and what to them was a good image. One section of the test pictured Caucasian, black, Asian, and Native American adults. The teacher asked each child to point out the person he wanted to be like when he grew up. Aaron spent quite a while studying those pictures, then selected a black man," Myrna said, hastening to add that this did not mean Aaron has a problem with whiteness.

Rather, Myrna believes Aaron has accepted Clifford as a father image. "But he also knows very well that he has a biological father who is white. He proved that one day when we were in a department store and Clifford was watching the kids while I tried on a dress. Aaron got separated from Clifford and was wandering around trying to find him. While I was in the dressing room, I heard Aaron asking for Clifford. The clerk wanted to know who Clifford was. 'He's my daddy,' Aaron said. 'What does he look like?' the clerk wanted to know. 'Well, he's big and he's black,' Aaron said, and I could imagine that clerk's face. You could almost hear her gulp through the dressing room walls. And I knew Aaron sensed that the woman was having problems understanding the situation, so he said very clearly and patiently: 'Oh, yes, he's my daddy. I have a black daddy and a white daddy.'"

Another custody case similar to Myrna's reached the Supreme Court after a Florida judge ruled, in the early 1980s, that a white mother should not be allowed custody of her three-year-old daughter. The mother had also married a black man following the divorce from her child's white father. In this case, the judge's decision was based on the view that there would be "pressures and stresses" on the child plus "social stigmatization" because of being part of an interracial family.

The Florida court decision was appealed and the Supreme Court ruled unanimously in April 1984 that "racial prejudice has no place in child custody determinations." Chief Justice Warren E. Burger, writing for the court, said that there was no justification for the Florida judge's action. Justice Burger cited the Equal Protection Clause of the U.S. Constitution, which forbids discriminatory actions by government.

Yet, it may be some time before the high court decision has any real impact on racial matching practices. Because of racist beliefs and the myths that only "like-race" families are constructive and healthy units for children, there likely will be continued attempts to award custody on the basis of matching children with "like-race" parents. In addition, some members of racial and ethnic groups believe that racial/ethnic matching is essential for the preservation of certain cultures.

The issue also goes beyond divorced, separated, and "remade" families. Members of interracial families formed by adoption or foster care describe in the next chapter how the controversy over racial matching has affected their lives.

TRANSRACIAL ADOPTION

8

*When people first meet me and
my biracial child, I'm often
aware of negative reactions—the
discomfort—people not knowing
what to say. Sometimes I'm ignored
or treated as if I'm a 'low-life.'
When these same people learn
that I am an adoptive parent of
a biracial child, their attitude
changes. Then I'm seen as a
humanitarian or something.
I really resent that attitude.*

White adoptive mother

I was born in Grand Rapids, Michigan. At the age of nearly three, I was placed in the Michigan Child Care System for adoption. During my ten-year stay in this system, I lived in ten different foster homes and two orphanages. I was adopted at twelve-and-a-half by my present family. . . .

One of the reasons I stayed in the system for so long is that I am what is called 'biracial." My birth mother is Dutch, French, German, and Polish. My birth father is Afro-American and American Indian. The Child Welfare System determined me to be a black child and stated that I must be placed in a black adoptive home. However, after ten years of no family wanting me, they settled for a white couple [and] that family today has six children. Three of them are white and were born to my parents. The other three are multiethnic and were adopted.

I haven't suffered from an identity crisis as a result of living with a white family. Actually, I have a very strong sense of my ethnicity, due to the efforts of my adoptive parents. They felt it was very important for me to know about all the cultures making up my background. They moved to an ethnically mixed neighborhood and cultivated a close and ethnically diverse circle of friends. . . .

Today, I see myself as a woman who is capable of fitting into any ethnic or cultural setting in the world. I personally am very happy that someone finally crossed color lines to adopt me. I don't feel that I've lost anything by being a part of this family.

I do, however, resent the fact that the then-used and still-practiced policy of "color matching" prevented me from having a family for ten years and wasted years of my life.

Sandra Illilonga, Detroit, Michigan[13]

The excerpt above is from testimony before a 1985 U.S. Senate committee that held hearings on barriers to adoption. According to Sandra, who is now in her thirties, and the testimony of others involved in child advocacy groups, hundreds of thousands of children have been denied temporary or permanent homes because of color-matching and ethnic-matching practices by placement agencies.

Interracial families formed by adoption are known in social work and social science jargon as "transracial adoptive families." Usually such families are formed when white parents adopt children who are biracial, black, Asian, Native American or Hispanic.

Transracial adoptions were fairly common in the 1960s because the number of white infants available for adoption had been steadily dropping. That trend continues, for several reasons: (1) an increasing number of unwed white mothers have been keeping their children, rather than giving them up for adoption; (2) more unwed women who become pregnant are having abortions; and (3) many women are practicing birth control, and thus are not having children.

With heightened racial/ethnic pride during the late sixties and early seventies, various minority groups began to oppose transracial adoptions—especially white families adopting nonwhite children. Native American groups, for example, have long been concerned about the large number of Native American children adopted by white parents. Many Native Americans believe white social workers make few attempts to place Native American children with tribal families because the families may have a different lifestyle from most middle-class American families.

Native American children are taught to value human relationships as opposed to being highly competitive. Older people have a place of respect, and age is considered a "badge of honor." Children are included in most extended-family social activities, and the idea of sharing with the larger family is stressed. Physical punishment is seldom used to discipline children in Native American families. Even correcting children in a loud voice is inappropriate.

These factors may be seen by white social workers as "weaknesses" rather than family strengths. Or the informal care of children by many extended family members could be viewed by those unfamiliar with Native American life as "unstructured" or even "dysfunctional"—a family form that does not adequately provide for children. Yet, Native American families may be quite capable of caring not only for biological children but also for adopted children. In the view of a number of recent researchers, Native American parent-child relationships are often stronger and healthier than those of the majority society.[14]

Along with Native Americans, black groups also have been concerned about transracial adoptions. In 1972, the National Association of Black Social Workers (NABSW) expressed "vehement opposition" to placing black children and black/white biracial children with white adopting families. This view was recently reinforced by William Merritt, president of the NABSW, in testimony before the 1985 Senate committee investigating adoption procedures. Merritt said that the NABSW has "an ethnic, moral and professional obligation to oppose transracial adoption. We are therefore *legally* justified in our efforts to protect the rights of black children, black families, and the black community. We view the placement of black children in white homes as a hostile act against our community. It is a blatant form of race and cultural genocide."

Other black social workers have pointed out that one of the reasons for the concerted effort to place children with parents of their own race is to protect past errors of judgment. As one agency worker explained it: "Black families have too often been regarded as 'unfit' for foster care or for adopting children. Sometimes the only reason for this assessment is that the family does not have the same life-style or income level as the 'idealized' middle-class white family used as a model for placement."

Another problem with placing black children with white families has to do with identity. Professor Joyce A. Ladner, sociologist at Howard University's School of Social Work, found in her 1977 study on black/white transracial adoption that some white parents can be naive about racial differences. Dr. Ladner explained that some parents did not consider color important and insisted that they had adopted "human beings" rather than children who are "black" or "part black." The parents refused to discuss the issue of black identity, believing that love is all that matters, and, that as parents, their prime concern should be developing healthy, secure individuals.

However, as with interracial parents and their biracial children, love *by itself* is not enough, Ladner contends. "It is possible for the parents to convey to their children that they, themselves, do not judge and relate to people on the basis of their skin color, but they should also tell the child that many people in the society do. Failure to do this will obviously leave the child unprepared to understand and deal with the first time he or she is called 'nigger' or some other racial slur," Ladner wrote.[15]

Black children adopted by white parents tend to have positive self-images as black persons *if* they live in integrated areas and if parents have helped their children understand that racial heritage is a source of pride. At least those are some of the conclusions reached in a study conducted by University of Texas social workers.

However, another recent study of several hundred adoptive families found little significance in racial identity. Published in the December 1984 issue of *Social Service*

Review, the study compared transracial adoptees—Latin American, Korean, and black—with white adoptees, all adopted by white families. After six years in their adopted families, the transracial adoptees appeared as well-adjusted as white adoptees.

In some cases, black adoptees in white families did not adjust well. But the evidence suggested that poor adjustment was related to the fact that black adoptees had been waiting longer than other adoptees for placement and often had moved from one foster home to another. The researchers could find no support for the argument that transracially adopted children in white homes will suffer psychological problems. Instead, the study pointed out that black and other minority children who are *not* placed in permanent homes can suffer considerable damage.[16]

There has been much media attention recently on the traumas generated by long waits for adoption and the shuffling of children around to various foster families that occur in order to achieve racial or ethnic matching. Much of the publicity has come about because of civil rights complaints against several state Departments of Social Services (DSS). State committees affiliated with the National Coalition to End Racism in America's Child Care System (NCERACCS) have accused social service departments of discrimination. DSS policies, it is charged, prevent adoption across color or ethnic lines. According to title VI of the Civil Rights Act of 1964, it is unlawful for any agency (such as a DSS) that receives federal funds to discriminate on the basis of race, color, or national origin.

In late 1985, the Michigan affiliate of NCERACCS was one of the plaintiffs in a Federal lawsuit brought against the Michigan DSS. Attorney Robert Sedler filed the suit on behalf of the committee and foster parents James and Margaret Quinn of Dearborn Heights, Michigan, who sought the committee's help. The Quinns are white and had been caring for two-and-a-half-year-old Corey, a black child, for fourteen months when the DSS took him from their home. Prior to that time, Corey had been in five homes and was placed in two more foster homes after being removed from the Quinns' home.

The Quinns charged, in their lawsuit, that the DSS removed Corey from their care for the prime purpose of placing him in a black foster home, a home which a news report claimed had an expired foster-care license. In addition, "the gas heat was cut off, mortgage payments were overdue, and a convicted felon lived there," the news story said.[17]

The Quinns tried to get Corey back, claiming that the DSS did not adhere to its own regulations, which state that foster parents who care for a child for more than a year are bonded to that child (they become the psychological parents of the child). In such cases, the DSS has ruled a child should not be removed from a foster home unless a permanent home is found.

After the complaint was filed, Corey was returned to the Quinns' home. Then, in March 1986, the court case was decided in favor of the Quinns. According to the court ruling, race may be only one of a number of factors that must be considered when determining the best interests of children placed in foster and adoptive families.

Attorney Sedler explained to a *Detroit Free Press* reporter: "There are far more black children in need of foster care in Michigan than there are black foster parents. What was happening in practice is that they (DSS) would make an ongoing placement with a white foster family and the placement was going well. As soon as a black foster home became available, they would yank the child solely on the basis of race. We argued that that was an unconstitutional or negative use of racial criteria."

Carol Coccia of Taylor, Michigan, president of NCERACCS (and founder of the Michigan committee), says the recent federal court decision should have precedent-setting impact on the national child care system. Coccia explained that NCERACCS has "heard from almost every state that minority kids are not getting placed. While the national committee's stance is that recruitment of foster and adoptive families, including minority families, should continue, children should not be denied placements due to lack of 'matching families.' "

Along with legal and publicity efforts by such groups as NCERACCS, many individuals are beginning to speak out on some of the traumas suffered by adoptive and foster care children and parents affected by "matching" practices. As Bernice Rigby of Detroit describes her experience: "It really did something to me!"

In 1981, Fred and Bernice Rigby accepted a one-and-a-half-year-old boy, a ward of the court, for long-term foster care that would include special medical attention for the boy. As foster parents, the Rigbys were told they would be able to keep the child as long as they wished and that they would have first consideration for adoption. Two years later, the youngster was available for adoption and the Rigbys applied. The couple qualified in all ways— except one. They were black and the child they wanted to adopt was white. The Rigbys were not allowed to adopt their foster son.

For a while the Rigbys were bitter and vowed never to take another white child for foster care. They did not want to be hurt again. But as Mrs. Rigby put it: "I can't do that to someone who needs help." She added, sadly, such an experience points up that "the racial thing is still here."

An adoptive parent in California agrees. Jean Izon of Los Angeles says: "Two of my daughters are black/white and one is Filipino/white. My husband (Filipino descent) and I (Anglo) were told by all local public and private agencies that we could only adopt a child who was a Filipino/white. They told us there was legislation in California which prevented a child of any other racial group (including other Asian nationalities) from being placed with us. We adopted through an international agency and now have a Korean son. We have since inquired about a ten-year-old Korean/white boy [and] we were told the agency would search the entire U.S. for a Korean/white couple before considering our request."

Nevertheless, the director of the California DSS has stated that "There is no legislative authority to prohibit transracial placements." The director also insists there is no ethnic-matching policy. But as Mrs. Izon points out, the practice continues in California and in most other states.

"We are seeing sibling groups of black and Hispanic children languishing in foster care for years on end while Anglo families are turned away from consideration," reported a Texas parent. In New York, a white couple was "outraged" when two years after they applied to adopt biracial youngsters the boys were still being held in group homes, waiting for "like-race" adoption. From Louisiana came a report that an eleven-year-old white girl was "seized as she got off the school bus"—taken from the care of foster black parents, in spite of the girl's wish to remain in her foster home. The girl had been with her foster parents for three years while her mother was in prison.

Because of the many barriers to adopting transracially in the United States, many families have turned to international agencies. That is, they have adopted children from continents and nations where requirements are less stringent and the waiting time shorter. Yet, there are some fifty thousand American children available for adoption each year. Less than half are actually adopted because they are older, handicapped, or children of color. Black American children make up the bulk of "waiting children."

Annette and Richard Hesters, who work a large dairy farm in northern Indiana, are among the many white parents who have adopted children from other countries as well as from the United States. The Hesters have five transracially adopted children and four biological offspring

Above: *Annette and Richard Hesters, who work a large
dairy farm in northern Indiana, are among the many
white parents who have adopted children from other
countries as well as transracially from within
the United States.* Below: *Annette with Tuan*

who are grown. Jeramy, the youngest adopted child, is Jamaican/American black, Terence is black/Puerto Rican, Tuan is Vietnamese, Tiffany is American black/white, and Teresa is Korean/black.

"All these social workers who claim that black adopted children won't identify as being black are just foolish," says Annette Hesters. "Our adopted daughter, Teresa, came to us when she was thirteen—her mother gave her up when she was twelve and that has created some resentment—psychological problems—which have nothing to do with skin color. Teresa is now nineteen and has joined the Army, where she is involved with blacks primarily. She still carries a lot of hostility and resentment around, but again it has to do with being given up by her Korean mother. She's been in for counseling in the Army and we believe in time she will work it out."

Tuan, who is thirteen, was adopted by the Hesters when he was just sixteen months old. Does Tuan have any thoughts about being "different" and having non-Asian parents? "Not really," he said. "I know that my mom and dad really wanted me. Besides I'm too busy with homework and chores—I take care of and milk a herd of goats. And I'm in the school band."

How do the other adopted children see themselves? Tiffany says she thinks of herself as tan. "That's because I'm part white and part black," she explained. Terence and Jeramy are too young to verbalize their sense of identity, but that hardly seems an issue with any of the Hesters. Rather, they are much more involved with daily life, coping with such everyday tasks as doing the dishes, feeding the dogs, or planning for a summer barbecue. Or there are arguments about which TV program to watch, or which crayons to use in a coloring book. And there are eyeglasses to fit, allergies to worry about, school functions to attend, bills to pay, tax forms to make out. In short, the Hesters are trying to function, as most families would like to do, in a healthy, constructive manner. Questions of racial identity are matters of interest but not a source of major trauma.

That's how Mark Steinmetz of South Bend, Indiana, sees it, too. The fourteen-year-old adopted son of Bob and Joan Steinmetz says, "Whenever somebody asks me what race I am, I always say both black and white or just Mixed. I consider myself half and half. Everybody just accepts that. I can't ever remember being upset or bothered by being 'different.' I don't think of myself that way. I've been in my family so long that sometimes I forget my dark color isn't the same as my parents and my younger sister and older brother. I'm just with them—you know—they're my family. I also spend a lot of time next door with a black family, and I get along with both blacks and whites. Our neighborhood and school are integrated and we just don't have problems around here."

"Whenever somebody asks me what race I am, I always say black and white or just Mixed."—Mark Steinmetz, age 14, adopted (Mark with his sister, Ruth.)

Mark's parents, both of whom have education degrees (Bob is an elementary school teacher), agree that there just haven't been problems for their son that stem from his black/white heritage or from being with others in the family who are white. As Joan explained it: "There have been growing-up problems, the typical teenage traumas, and Mark has certainly tested us to see if we love him as much as our biological children. That's what a lot of adopted kids do. But we don't feel he has had any problems directly related to being biracial in a white family."

Another South Bend family with three transracially adopted children agrees that problems are not necessarily race-related. Although, as Greg, a black/white biracial junior high student pointed out: "We had a bad time on the school bus for a while because the bus driver didn't like me and my sister, Keana. (Keana is of Korean/black parentage and a year older than her brother.) The bus driver was a black lady and she kept asking us about our family and who that white man was standing at the corner with us. We said he was our dad and she got all upset. She used to get mad because we'd be with white friends and pick on us all the time—say mean things. I guess she didn't think black kids ought to be with whites or something. It's not like that now because we have a different bus driver."

Although many nonwhite children who are adopted by white parents seem to function in a healthy manner, they may also be victims of racism and can have problems with self-identity during their development years. Lisa Zang, of Chinese ancestry, was adopted by Ellen and Jack Zang of Chicago when she was a toddler. While growing up, Lisa would often stare at herself in the mirror and carefully examine her eyes, then tell her mother, "I wish my eyes would be like yours."

At the same time, a younger sister, a biological child, would pull at her eyes, trying to make them look like Lisa's. But that "didn't make Lisa feel any better," Ellen Zang reported. "Lisa often seemed to reject people who looked like her. We had Chinese friends who would come to visit but Lisa would run away and hide until they left. In later years, though, we met another Asian couple—Japanese/Korean—and when they came to visit, Lisa would curl up beside the woman, as if she saw her as a kind of 'Oriental mother'—certainly more of a mirror of herself than I could be. As our friendship with that couple grew, Lisa seemed to accept her Chinese identity."

A few studies have shown that the vast majority of Asian adolescents adopted by American families seldom think of themselves in terms of their Asian ancestry.[18] This could be detrimental. According to some behavior experts, if children of Asian ancestry try to deny their heritage and think of themselves as "like-white" or the same as their adopted parents, they may be headed for psychological problems related to self-identity. Thus family counselors urge adoptive white parents to provide opportunities for the children of Asian ancestry to learn about various aspects of their heritage.

John and Cathy Bair of Niles, Michigan, have made efforts to help their adopted daughter, Callie, of Korean ancestry, achieve a positive self-identity. As a family they have made it a practice to attend a Korean Lions Picnic held every summer in Chicago. The all-day event includes food, dances, music, and other entertainment that reflects the Korean culture. However, Cathy Bair admits this once-a-year outing might not be enough to help her daughter learn about her ancestry. But, at the moment, Callie has not expressed any need to identify with Korean culture or to "feel Korean," her mother reports, and "we have often talked about differences in people—from an early age I've tried to explain to her that no two individuals are alike any more than flowers, birds, and other living things are exactly alike. So there is no need to feel uncomfortable about being 'different'—in fact, it's special."

Very little research has been conducted to determine

"When people ask us what we are we usually say we are Spanish."—Marisa and Jacqui Smucker, both age 14, adopted

whether Latin American children adopted into white homes have problems related to identity. But certainly many Hispanics are faced with prejudice because of having a language, culture, and physical appearance different from the white majority.

Teenagers Jacqui and Marisa of Costa Rica, who are of black/Hispanic heritage, were adopted by a white family and live in a rural all-white area in Indiana. The girls say they have sometimes been asked about their heritage and usually explain that they are Spanish. But a few kids at school have called them "niggers." "We haven't had a lot of trouble with name-calling," Marisa said, "and it doesn't bother me too much anyway because I know myself well enough and I like who I am."

Once again, whether a person is part of an adopted or a biological interracial family, racism seems to be the ugliest barrier to acceptance in the majority white society.

Still, that is not the only conflict, as pointed out earlier in arguments about racial or cultural identity. And such arguments cannot be easily dismissed.

Sally Caldwell, an adoptive mother of a Native Alaskan child, tried to put the issue in perspective. The Caldwell's infant was placed in their "non-native family" by their son's birth mother, an unwed Eskimo woman in her twenties. The woman had been raised in foster care, not in her village. But according to the Indian Child Welfare Act (ICWA), the woman's parents and the tribe of her parents as well as the tribe of the village where the woman was raised had to be notified of the pending adoption. An attorney representing the parent's tribe contested the adoption and proposed that the child be placed with the maternal grandparents.

In Eskimo and other Native American cultures, such action is appropriate. The rights of the individual are sacrificed for the rights of the group when the health and well-being of the group are threatened. Mrs. Caldwell explained that the court had to determine whether placing a Native Alaskan child in a home outside the tribal group violated ICWA provisions.

The Native American mother filed depositions with the court indicating she wanted the baby in the Caldwell home and not with her parents. Still, the tribal group has the right to self-determination, which means "the group determines what is in the best interest of the group based on its own value system," Mrs. Caldwell said. But the birth mother asserted her rights and convinced her parents and the tribal group to withdraw their petition to intervene—that is, to no longer object to placing the baby in a "non-native" family. So the adoption could be finalized.

Yet, Mrs. Caldwell went on to underscore a point at issue in many crosscultural relationships. She asks whether "the rights of the child are to be preferred" over the group's rights, and if so, is that decision "in conflict with the basic value system of another culture?"[19] In other words, will minority cultures be undermined or destroyed if adopted children or biological children of interracial families are raised with the values of the dominant/majority white culture?

The question is one of the underlying factors along with racism in the ongoing controversy over interracial families, whether formed by adoption, by remarriage, or intermarriage.

SUPPORT GROUPS

*As a slave, my mother was forced
to "mix" and breed and no one
would even think, let alone worry,
about the child she had conceived
because of a white "master."
My mother killed that child.*

Elderly black woman
in Cleveland, Ohio

Another issue that often comes up in regard to interracial families is how to raise healthy biracial or mixed children in an unhealthy society. This is a question that has been posed in national and regional conferences on interracial families. It is also a question that is basic to many support groups that have emerged across the nation. Not because members of interracial and interethnic families have so many problems, but because a racist society tries to degrade, and thus creates problems for, such families.

Networks of interracial and intercultural families share positive approaches to parenting their children. Group members also compile objective information and historical material about their particular family structures.

Janine Brown, active in the Interracial Family Alliance of Atlanta, Georgia, pointed out that "Interracial families are basically like most other families, but they sometimes lack family and community support systems. Because of the shortage of objective informational materials about interracial families, parents may also need guidance in how to help their biracial children develop self-esteem. So our network in Atlanta—like others in the nation—was set up in response to these needs and to promote public acceptance of the interracial family unit as a healthy family structure in our society."

Other network groups echo such views. And most have set some specific goals for their organizations. Some concentrate on religious objectives. For example, Interracial Families, Inc., in Tarentum, Pennsylvania, is a nonprofit

Christian social service agency serving the Pittsburgh area. Its director, Charles Stewart, Jr., a minister and social worker who is interracially married, says the group provides counseling for interracial families confronted with problems of racism or problems of a spiritual nature. Another religious support group, in Gardena, California, is called "A Place for Us" Ministry for Interracial Couples. The founders, Steve and Ruth White, say one of their main concerns is to break down barriers of prejudice and racism within the churches.

Most interracial groups, however, have secular purposes, such as establishing pride in racial identity. I-Pride, which stands for Interracial/Intercultural Pride, states that one of its main purposes "is to validate people of multiple heritage within the context of 'pride.'" The group, founded in 1979 in the San Francisco Bay area, includes interracial and intercultural families (biological and adoptive), multiracial adults, educators, social workers, therapists, and others interested in the well-being of children and families of more than one ethnic or cultural heritage. Members are involved in activities that range from publishing a newsletter and conducting educational workshops on multiracial children and adults to providing support for interracial and intercultural families.

Along with local support, certain groups also keep up a network of information across the nation. This could take the form of providing interracial families who are planning to move with information about a new location. For example, if a family is relocating from New York to Texas, the Interracial Family Alliance in Houston might be able to suggest which city neighborhoods and areas around Houston are hospitable to interracial families. National networking is also a good way for interracial families to learn about new materials on parenting that fit their particular family structure or to just meet other interracial families. "If an interracial family plans a visit to Washington, D.C., they might want to contact the Interracial

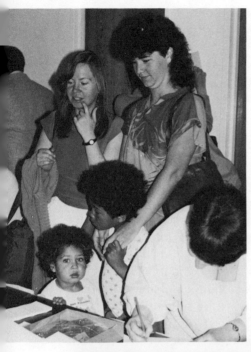

I-Pride, an interracial/ intercultural support group based in the San Francisco Bay area, recently hosted a national conference on the children of interracial families sponsored by the Council on Interracial Books for Children.

Family Circle and take part in our activities," suggests Lynne Bobbitt, president of that organization.

As with most other interracial support groups, the Interracial Family Circle (IFC) in the Washington, D.C.– Baltimore area was founded by a few interracial parents who gathered to discuss their own needs and those of other interracial families in their local area.

Ed and Emma Tarleton, who initiated the first gathering of IFC members in 1984, are the only interracial couple in their Maryland community. They felt their black/white biracial child, Heather, would be isolated if she did not have the opportunity to be with other biracial children. Thus, the Tarletons were motivated to contact other interracial families and help organize and formally establish IFC.

Other support groups may come about because of concerns that transracial adoptive families share. Still others serve interracial families headed by single parents. A few organizations, such as INTERace in Flushing, New York, have affiliated groups that offer activities geared for teenagers.

Support groups sometimes grow quickly, especially when news spreads about an organization. But groups carefully preserve the privacy of their members. Most use post office box numbers for their organization addresses and some make use of phone answering machines to help screen calls. As one member of a support group noted: "You never know what kind of kook is out there wanting to harass or really do physical harm. In some areas you don't have to worry about stuff like that. But in others there could be people out to vent their hatred on anyone different from themselves."

For the most part, though, interracial and intercultural family groups stress the positive, not the negative. Many members of interracial families are making themselves known in order to help sensitize others in the society to the special needs and interests of multiracial children.

Education, they feel, is the key to breaking down racial barriers.

The Biracial Family Network in Chicago, for example, printed ten objectives for its membership. Among them were several educational goals: to encourage members to research and be proud of all their roots; to give children a scientific background on their inherited characteristics that are used for racial identification; and to find experts and resource materials on the subject of racial mixing and interracial families.

Bringing together experts and calling attention to constructive resources are some of the main purposes of national and regional conferences on interracial and intercultural families. The first national conference for interracial families was held in New York City in 1984 and was sponsored by the Council on Interracial Books for Children (CIBC). Other annual CIBC-sponsored conferences have followed. Although the New York–based CIBC is mainly concerned about racism, sexism, and other forms of bias in various media and in institutions such as schools, the conferences have helped call attention to the few materials that reflect the reality of interracial families.

Kate Shackford, codirector with Emily Leinster of the conferences, pointed out in a 1984 CIBC *Bulletin* that "interracial families—which have a high visibility in our society—are virtually invisible in literature, curricula and the media. When interracial children open storybooks and textbooks, they find no families like their own; for the publishing world, they are invisible."

The situation has changed little since 1984. Thus many members of support groups often shape ideas about how to create their own books, toys, games, and other educational materials that will reflect their children's biracial identity.

Another important function of interracial family conferences and support groups is providing the opportunity for families to meet in a warm and friendly environment where they will not be shunned or looked upon as "abnormal" or as "low-life" or somehow "immoral." The fact is, parents in interracial families, whether biological, stepparents, or adoptive, whether single or part of a married couple, are often highly conscious of their responsibilities as parents. Most are more aware of the need to develop skills in communication and human relationships than are members of "like-race" families.

As a result, there appears to be more openness and willingness to cooperate and to make family units function in healthy and constructive ways. Perhaps this is because interracial and intercultural families know how difficult it is to work through, on their own, ways to deal with the deeply rooted racism that affects all people in our nation.

Often interracial parents investigate schools and inquire about the racial attitudes of teachers and administrators—efforts which in themselves may alert educators to their own prejudicial behaviors. Some families just by their presence in a community may also point out to care givers—social workers, health professionals, and others—that people of multiracial backgrounds need supportive resources.

Just by being themselves, interracial and intercultural families also enhance a community and are a valuable asset. Their "rainbow effect" could well be a model for the majority of families in our nation. Certainly children and adults "of the rainbow" can be positive symbols of harmony.

Ramona Douglass, who wrote recently that she is "'Black' and 'White' and 'Brown' all over"[20] because she was born of an Italian American mother and an Afro-American Indian father, pointed out that "To be multiracial is to possess an extraordinary gift, for incorporated within me and others like me is living proof that colors and races can mix harmoniously—beautifully—completely—

denying or detracting from nothing and no one. And maybe, just maybe, through that mixing, race will some-day become just another four-letter word with no emotional charge or petty significance."

NOTES

Chapter One

1. Geiger, Geoff, "The Journey From 'Other'," *I-Pride Newsletter*, April 1986, Vol. 8, No. 2, p. 1.

Chapter Two

2. *Valley News Dispatch,* Philadelphia, PA, November 22, 1985.
3. Becker, John T. and Stanli K. *All Blood Is Red . . . All Shadows Are Dark.* Cleveland, Ohio: Seven Shadows Press, p. 5.
4. "Children of the Rainbow," *Newsweek,* November 19, 1984, p. 122.

Chapter Three

5. Derman-Sparks, Louise, "Dealing with Racial Slurs," *Interracial Books for Children* BULLETIN, Vol. 11, Nos. 3&4, 1980, pp 17-18.
6. Ibid.

Chapter Four

7. Hesslink, George K. *Black Neighbors: Negroes in a Northern Rural Community.* The Bobbs-Merrill Company, Inc., New York: 1974.

Chapter Six

8. Poussaint, Alvin F., "Study of Interracial Children Presents Positive Picture," *Interracial Books for Children* BULLETIN, Vol. 15, No. 6, 1984, pp. 9-10.
9. Remarks at a conference on Children of Interracial Families in Oakland, California, April 19-20, 1986.
10. Kich, George Kitahara, et al, "Interracial? Wakarimasen," reprinted in part in *I-Pride Newsletter*, Vol. 8, No. 2, April 1986, pp. 6-7.

Chapter Seven

11. Remarks at a conference on Children of Interracial Families in Oakland, California, April 19-20, 1986.
12. unpublished master's thesis

Chapter Eight

13. excerpt reprinted in NCERACC *Newsletter,* Vol. II, No. 2, July 1985. pp. 1-2.
14. Burgess, Bill J., ED.D., "Parenting in the Native-American Community," Chapter 6, pp. 63-73, *Parenting in a Multicultural Society,* New York: Longman, Inc., 1980.
15. Ladner, Joyce A., Ph.D. *Mixed Families: Adopting Across Racial Boundaries.* New York: Anchor Books/Doubleday, 1978, p. 125.
16. Feigelman, William and Silverman, Arnold R., "The Long-Term Effects of Transracial Adoption," *Social Service Review,* December 1984, pp. 588-602.
17. Daugherty, Jane, "State Agrees to Interracial Adoptions," *Detroit Free Press,* March 4, 1986, pp. 1A & 13A.
18. Feigelman, William and Silverman, Arnold R., "The Long-Term Effects of Transracial Adoption," *Social Service Review,* December 1984, pp. 588-602.
19. Letter from Sally Caldwell printed in *Newsletter* for the Committee to End Racism in Michigan's Child Care System, Inc., Vol. III, No. 2, August 1984, p. 3.

Chapter Nine

20. Douglass, Ramona, "What's Black and White and Brown All Over?", *The Interracial/Intercultureal* CONNECTION, Vol. 5, No. 3, May-June 1986, p. 1.

FOR FURTHER READING

Books

Acuña, Rodolfo. *Occupied America: The Chicanos' Struggle Toward Liberation.* New York: Harper & Row, 1972.

Becker, John T., and Stanli K. *All Blood Is Red . . . All Shadows Are Dark!* Seven Shadows Press, P.O. Box 1118, Cleveland, Ohio 44120.

Beuf, Ann. *Red Children in White America.* Philadelphia: University of Philadelphia Press, 1977.

Chen, Jack. *The Chinese of America.* New York: Harper & Row Publishers, Inc., 1980.

Comer, James, and Poussaint, Alvin. *Black Child Care: How to Bring Up a Healthy Black Child in America.* New York: Simon & Schuster, 1975.

Dunbar, Leslie W., ed. *Minority Report: What Has Happened to Blacks, Hispanics, American Indians, and Other Minorities in the Eighties.* New York: Pantheon Books, 1984.

Ehrlich, Paul R., and Feldman, Shirley S. *The Race Bomb: Skin Color, Prejudice, and Intelligence.* New York: Ballantine Books, 1977.

Fantini, Mario D., and Cárdenas, René, eds. *Parenting in a Multicultural Society.* New York: Longman, Inc., 1980.

Feigelman, William, and Silverman, Arnold R. *Chosen Children: New Patterns of Adoptive Relationships.* New York: Praeger, 1983.

Goodman, Mary Ellen. *Race Awareness in Young Children.* New York: Collier Books, 1952.

Hamilton, Virginia. *Arilla Sun Down.* New York: Greenwillow Press, 1976. (young adult novel)

Henriques, Fernando. *Children of Conflict: A Study of Interracial Sex and Marriage.* New York: Dutton, 1975.

Hernton, Calvin C. *Sex and Racism.* New York: Grove Press, 1966.

Katz, Judy. *White Awareness: Handbook for Anti-Racist Training.* Norman, OK: University of Oklahoma Press, 1978.

Katz, P. *Toward the Elimination of Racism.* New York: Pergamon Press, 1976.

Kitano, Harry. *Japanese Americans: The Evolution of a Subculture.* Englewood Cliffs, NJ: Prentice-Hall, 1969.

Ladner, Joyce A., Ph.D. *Mixed Families: Adopting Across Racial Boundaries.* Garden City, New York: Anchor Press/Doubleday, 1978.

Lindsey, Paul and Ouida. *Breaking the Bonds of Racism.* Palm Springs, CA: ETC Publications, 1974.

Martin, Elmer P. and Martin, Joanne Mitchell. *The Black Extended Family.* Chicago: University of Chicago Press, 1978.
Montagu, Ashley. *Man's Most Dangerous Myth: The Fallacy of Race.* New York: Oxford University Press, 1974.
Porterfield, Ernest. *Black and White Mixed Marriages: an Ethnographic Study of Black-White Families.* Chicago: Nelson-Hall, Inc., 1978.
Unger, Steven, ed. *The Destruction of American Indian Families.* New York: Association on American Indian Affairs, 1977.
Washington, Joseph R., Jr. *Marriage in Black and White.* Boston: Beacon Press, 1970.
Wilkinson, Doris Y. *Black Male/White Female: Perspectives on Interracial Marriage and Courtship.* Schenkman Publishing Company, Inc., Cambridge, MA 02138, 1975.

Periodicals

Amster, Sara-Ellen, "When Two Races Mix," *TeenAge*, March 1985, pp. 34–37.
Children of Interracial Families," *Bulletin*, Volume 15, Number 6, 1984 (entire issue), Council on Interracial Books for Children, Inc.
Children of the Rainbow," *Newsweek*, November 19, 1984, pp. 120–122.
Children, Race and Racism: How Race Awareness Develops," *Bulletin*, Volume 11, Numbers 3 and 4, 1980 (entire issue), Council on Interracial Books for Children, Inc.
Feigelman, William, and Silverman, Arnold R., "The Long-term Effects of Transracial Adoption," *Social Service Review*, December 1984, pp. 588–602.
Intermarriage in the United States," *Marriage and Family Review*, Volume 5, No. 1, Spring 1982 (entire issue).
Kevles, Barbara, "What It's Like to Be the Child of an Interracial Marriage," *Glamour*, January 1980, pp. 20–23.
McRoy, Ruth G., et al. "The Identity of Transracial Adoptees" *Social Casework: The Journal of Contemporary Social Work*, January 1984, pp. 34–39.
Norment, Lynn, "A Probing Look at Children of Interracial Marriages," *Ebony*, September 1985, pp. 155–162.

RESOURCE ORGANIZATIONS

*Concerned with
Interracial/Intercultural
Families and Children*

Biracial Family Network, P.O. Box 489, Chicago, IL 60653-0489

Biracial Family Resource Center, 800 Riverside Drive, New York, NY 10032

Council on Interracial Books for Children, Inc., 1841 Broadway, New York, NY 10023

INTERace, P.O. Box 7143, Flushing, NY 11352

Interracial Club of Buffalo, Box 146, Amherst Branch, Buffalo, NY 14226

Interracial Families, Inc. Dayspring Christian Center, 700 Second Ave., Tarentum, PA 15084

Interracial Family Alliance (IFA), P.O. Box 16248, Houston, TX 77222

Interracial Family Circle, P.O. Box 53290, Washington, DC 20009

I-Pride, 1060 Tennessee Street, San Francisco, CA 94107

National Coalition to End Racism in America's Child Care System, Inc., 22075 Koths, Taylor, MI 48180

National Committee For Adoption, 2025 M Street, N.W., Suite 512, Washington, DC 20036

New Race, Inc., P.O. Box 3071, Colorado Springs, CO 80934

OURS, Inc., 3307 Highway North, Minneapolis, MN 55422

Parenting for Peace & Justice, 4144 Lindell, #400, St. Louis, MO 63108

Parents of Interracial Children (PIC), 115 South 46th Street, Omaha, NB 68132

Rainbow Circle, c/o Broadfield Assoc., P.O. Box 242, Chester, PA 19016-0242

INDEX

ABOUT THE AUTHOR

Kathlyn Gay has written books, stories,
magazine features, and plays for both
young readers and adults. Her book
Acid Rain, published by Franklin Watts,
was cited by both the National Council
for Social Studies and the National
Science Teachers Association as one of
the notable children's books for 1983.

Ms. Gay and her husband, Arthur L. Gay,
live in Elkhart, Indiana.